Seeing Through the Dark

by Shelly Owen

"And this is my prayer: that your love may abound more and more in knowledge and depth of insight, so that you may be able to discern what is best and may be pure and blameless until the day of Christ."

-- Philippians 1:9-11

ISBN: 9781677593064

This book is dedicated to:

Yeshua, who reached into the pit of darkness and pulled me out into His marvelous light.
All I have is His, by Him and for Him. Without Him I am nothing.
I am humbled beyond words that He chose me.

My husband, David, and our two boys, James and Matthew
You guys have endured my absence as I wrote,
honored my time with the Lord as I prayed and researched,
and lovingly chose to let me write.
My heart is so full because of you guys!

Ruth Ann McDonald
You believed in me even when I didn't believe in myself.
You pushed me out even when I felt I wasn't ready, and trusted in me
enough to allow me to share.
You are far more than just my Apostolic covering, but a spiritual mother,
friend, and confidant.
I love you to the moon and back!

The intercessors who prayed me through this
You guys have been so faithful to pray and advise me of what the Lord was showing you.
I could not have completed this without your covering.
I am honored that you guys chose this assignment.

Cherie Bosch
You were so faithful to Lord to ask me the hard questions concerning this book and
praying with me to receive the downloads from Heaven so I could write the book.
May God return to you 100 fold what you poured into me.

Debra Mather and Angie Burks
Through everything, you two were unafraid
to allow the sparks to fly as you guys sharpened me.
You helped counsel, correct, and redirect me when I needed it.
Your friendship has changed me in deep ways.
I cannot imagine my life without the two of you.

Introduction

If the devil can ever rob you of spiritual knowings,
then you are left confused and defenseless.

--Roberts Lairdon

If you are reading this book, then you have taken up the call to grow and develop your discernment to the highest possible level and become more proficient in discernment. The purpose of this manual is to help train you in discernment. I realize this book is not going to be everyone's cup of tea. Some of the subjects may be disturbing and strange to some. You will notice I refer to Jesus as Yeshua. This is His Hebrew name. There is no disrespect intended to those who call Him Jesus. But if you hang in there, you will be armed to wage war in a new way in intercession.

Please note that this will be a sometimes painful journey as your gifting matures. One must count the cost before developing any new or already existing skillset. You must allow for mistakes and correction as well as for growth beyond what you thought was possible. Are you willing to pay the price of losing your selfish ambition, go into a place of deep intimacy with the Holy Spirit, and be thought of as weird by some? If so, keep reading.

As followers of Christ, we must be keenly aware of the spiritual realm at all times. It is the power of God that allows us to see through the dark and find Him everywhere. We must know from where the information and doctrines we are receiving are coming. Not only that, but we must be aware of the spirits at work in our day to day lives influencing our attitudes and actions. There will be some repetition within these pages to bring emphasis to a particular point. There are also application exercises to help you grow. Always cover yourself in prayer before each activity. Why? Covering yourself in prayer prevents things from attaching to you as well as shutting down your bloodline from interfering with you as you discern.

If you want to become good at something, you practice. The same is true for discernment. The Bible tells us in Hebrews 12:14 to practice our discernment. It is one of the ways we become mature. Chuck Pierce, president of Global Spheres, Inc., teaches that we should be discerning on a daily basis.[1] I could not agree more. Discernment has to be a way of life for the Christian. Discernment is more important than the air we breathe now more than ever. Our spiritual eyes need always to be open. That means 24/7 discernment.

Even in 24/7 discernment, we need balance. I used to hate to have my discernment going non-stop. It wore me out. I could not stand to go to Walmart for everything I was sensing. I begged God to make it stop or to at least turn it down a notch. Then one day, He did. I could not feel anything for over a month, and that's when I understood. I had allowed myself to get burned out. I had forgotten to do what Yeshua used to do. Before He would minister, we see time and time again in the Bible where Yeshua would slip away to the mountain and pray and be with His Father. In all of my running around, I failed to stop and ask the Father to guard my discernment and only allow me to sense what He wanted me to sense. I was going and going and going discerning everything with no buffer zone. It was maddening. As I began to do this, my discernment returned. There was a sense of peace and rest in it. I no longer fret over going to Walmart or the grocery store. I no longer get weirded out in parks with bizarre sculptures and statues. I stay in my lane and listen to the Holy Spirit. I focus on what He wants instead of every little demonic fuzz ball that goes scurrying by.

I need to warn you here. As you begin to operate in 24/7 discernment, you will start to see a lot. You will see things EVERYWHERE! Even in places you have been and never felt or sensed anything before. Pray and cover yourself as you learn. The Father will show you what is yours to battle and what is His. When you go out and about with your daily life, remember balance. Always look for Yeshua first. Ask the Lord to show you the divine angelic hosts around you. Always seek the heavenly first.

Take notes of what you see, hear, feel, taste, and smell. Do not be afraid to use your five physical senses. I will touch more on this later in this book. If you find yourself only experience the demonic as you discern, reach out immediately for inner healing and deliverance. Areas of wounding and generational issues are more than likely the culprit and will need to be addressed before you can be effective in the area of discernment.

My desire for this book is to share with you what I have learned to equip you on this journey of sharpening your discernment skills. I hope to teach you what discernment is and is not. To help guide you in the practice of daily discernment. To help you not make the mistakes I have. To open up your mind to what you can discern. This information may seem elementary and plain common sense to some; however, please pay careful consideration to what I have written in this manual. Even the most common of knowledge can sometimes be the very thing that trips us up. There **IS NO** room in discernment for *"know-it-alls."* Do not allow yourself to get puffed up in what you know or think about discernment, and as you begin to operate. It can be so easy to puff up as your discernment goes to a higher level. Be mindful of your own heart and do not allow pridefulness to overtake you giving place to the enemy. There is no room in discernment for assumptions or presumptions. The only thing you should know for sure is that you know absolutely nothing and are trusting God to reveal all you need to know. When used correctly, discernment becomes a mighty weapon in our arsenal.

I hope that you will be able to discern not just with your natural eyes, but with all of your natural senses as well. And, it will take some practice and patience. Sharpening and training take time. Give yourself grace as you develop your gift. All of the gifts operate by love, so ground yourself in the perfect love of God toward yourself and others as you grow.

Here is a list of helpful guidelines for you to follow as you develop your discernment. Now, take a deep breath and let's begin.

> ➤ ***Place prayer and worship as a top priority.*** Seeking the heart of the Father first will allow you to see what is going on in your surroundings. Always bathe yourself in prayer and deep intimate worship first before attempting to discern anything or anyone. This habit will be the regular precursor to all of the exercises we will do throughout this book.

- ➤ *Keep your Word life healthy.* Always stay in the Word of God. Our Heavenly Father reveals His character and His ways to us through His Word. The more you know the Word, the better you will know the Father and the sharper your discernment will be.

- ➤ *Find balance.* It is very easy to be caught up in the darkness we see and sense. We must find a balance between sensing the bad and the good. If we only see the bad, we can quickly become discouraged and stop using our discernment out of fear. Ask the Holy Spirit to fine-tune your discernment so you can experience God's angelic realm. Always seek the Light in all you do.

- ➤ *Practice.* The old saying "practice makes perfect" most definitely applies here. You can practice by yourself or find a mentor to help sharpen your ability.

- ➤ *Keep a discernment journal.* Keep track of what you see, feel, hear, taste, and smell each time so you will be aware of how your body reacts to both the Holy Spirit, the angels, and to the spirits of darkness. Writing down your sensory reactions, when encountering both the divine and the demonic, will help you keep track of how your body responds to what you have encountered. Each time you experience the a reaction, you can look back at your journal and verify what you are sensing. This journal will be your road map of sorts to your discernment.

- ➤ *Share what you are discerning appropriately.* Discernment is not to be used as a witch hunt or to gather gossip. Our gift is a warfare tool as well as for a shield of our church and spiritual community. Do not give place to gossip. Do not use what you are seeing or experiencing about a person or church body as an excuse to gossip or bash a person or ministry. Pray about what you see and only share with those you trust that will help you pray about what you have sensed.

- ➤ *Submit your gift to authority.* ALWAYS, ALWAYS (I cannot stress this enough), ALWAYS submit your gift to the authority of someone who has the spiritual rule over you. An example would be to submit what you feel or sense to your pastor or church leadership before releasing what you are discerning to the church body where you are a member.

- > *Trust your instincts and ability to discern.* Do not place doubts in what you are feeling in the physical or seeing in the spirit realm. The enemy would love nothing more than to cause you to doubt your ability and stop using discernment.

- > *Always keep yourself in check.* Keep in mind that your emotional and spiritual state will significantly impact your discernment. You can command your emotions, in the name of Yeshua, to take a back seat to your spirit man while you are discerning. If you have unforgiveness towards someone, it will affect your discernment. We must strive to the best of our abilities to be pure vessels fit for the Master's use.

- > *Do not be afraid of telling the truth.* The truth can hurt, but it can also be freeing. Do not be afraid to admit you are not sensing, hearing, or feeling anything. Take it as the Father shielding you from something that you may not be able to process mentally or spiritually.

- > *Be humble.* Always use your gift with humility. It is very easy to feel like you have something someone else does not. Remember, pride comes before a fall. Always check yourself before releasing what you sense.

- > *Don't compare.* Do not compare the way you discern to another. Your discernment is as unique as you are, you have no rival. No two people will discern something the same way. Your discernment is as individual as you are. Embrace your differences, and do not focus on the person standing next to you.

- > *Seek inner healing.* Do not forget to seek inner healing. We all have things happen throughout our lives. Life leaves us scarred. It is imperative to seek healing if you want to discern at higher levels. Our woundings and generational iniquities cloud our spiritual vision and plug up our spiritual ears. Deliverance will look different for each of you. Seek it like precious gold.

The following is an example prayer of how to close off your bloodline and cover yourself before discerning. Just as Yeshua laid out a structure for prayer for us in Matthew 6:9-15, let this prayer serve as a model for you to build off of and to create your own prayer.

Father God, I praise You and lift my voice in worship to You. I thank You, Father, for the opportunity to serve You in the area of discernment. I come before You and present my discernment to You. I ask that You purify my senses so that I may glorify You and see what You want me to see during this time. I ask for the ability to judge clearly what is of You and what is not. Help me to see through the dark. I call my senses under the subjection of the Holy Spirit, now in the name of Yeshua.

I also lift my bloodline up to You, Father. I ask that any, and all, doors be closed off to my generations so they will not interfere with my discernment. I apply the blood of Yeshua to every doorpost and lintel of my generations so they will not be an opening for the enemy to attack or distract me. I cover my mind, will, and emotions under the blood of Yeshua. I speak to my emotions and say you cannot speak to, for, against, with, or about me in the spiritual realm. You are silenced in Yeshua's name. I bind, in Yeshua's name, any ungodly watchers assigned to my bloodline and say you are blind, deaf, and mute. They will not report anything to their master. Help me, Yeshua, to see You in the midst of everything that I experience when I discern.

Lord Yeshua, I ask that You cover me, my finances, my family, and all that pertains to me in Your precious blood. Hide me under the shadow of Your wings and behind the veil of the Holy Spirit so that I am not seen, heard, felt, or otherwise experienced by the enemy or his agents. Make me mindful of my thoughts as I discern so that they will not hinder me as I use my discernment. I take captive every thought into the obedience of Yeshua now! I declare I have the mind of Christ. I think through Him. I perceive through and by Yeshua.

I ask, Father God, for all distractions, whether they be in the natural or in the spirit, to cease and desist in Yeshua's name. Nothing will cause me to get off course as I discern. I declare that I have clear spiritual vision. Father, increase my ability to see past any barriers to my spiritual vision the enemy would place before me. I see only what You want me to see in Yeshua's name.

Thank You, Father, for Your divine protection and provision as I discern. I honor You with my gift and bless Your Holy Name. Thank You, Yeshua, for being with me and guiding me as I discern.

Table of Contents:

Section 1 – Discernment 101

Section 2 – Next Level Discernment

"The Word of God is the basis for all discernment." – Roberts Lairdon

Section 1

Discernment 101

Chapter One
What Discernment Is and is Not

"Discernment intersects the Christian life at every point." – *John MacArthur*

Before we can adequately understand discernment and be trained therein, we must first fully grasp what discernment is and is not. There is a lot of confusion surrounding discernment. Many misuse this gift bringing harm and damage to the Body of Christ. When used correctly, it builds and protects individual believers as well as the Body. Discernment has become something of a misconception within the Church. Highly discerning people can come across as prideful, aloof, loners, and judgmental. Most Western Christian denominations have stifled discernment and boxed it in to only knowing whether or not the preached doctrine is the truth from the Word of God. But, discernment is multifaceted and goes way deeper than just that. Discernment is first and foremost designed to bring us to a place of intimacy with the Father through intercession.

What Discernment Is

So what is discernment? The definition will vary depending on who you ask. Some might say only the *"spiritual elite"* have it or that it is something mystics walk in. Some might say discernment is only for church settings.

The Merriam-Webster dictionary defines discernment as *"the quality of being able to grasp and comprehend what is obscure: skill in discerning, an act of perceiving or discerning something."* In a nutshell, discernment is the in-born ability to determine whether something is good or bad. It is the inner knowing within us all that something is more than meets the eye. It is the ability to see beyond face value and through the dark.

We can pick up on emotions just by watching facial expressions. We can observe the eyes and body language to tell when someone is lying. You can read someone's character by their actions and attitudes. You can also pick up on someone's inner turmoil by just being in their presence. This ability is what I call *"practical discernment."* This type of discernment comes from your human spirit. Christian Author Roberts Lairdon refers to this as *"daily discernment."* Practical discernment is the type of discernment the occult has learned and is light years ahead of the church in. They eat, sleep, live, and breathe it.

Have you ever wondered why some detectives are so good at their jobs? It's like they have a sixth sense that enables them to know things. They can see things others cannot. They have trained themselves to see the clues in front of them and recognize how they go together. When asked about it, most detectives will tell you it is a *"gut feeling"* they have. They have trained their discernment and just termed it something else.

Have you ever noticed some born-again believers seem to just instinctively know where to go, who to see, and what to say when they get there? It is through their intimacy with the Holy Spirit that these believers have built a clear line of communication between their spirit and the Father. If you ask them, they will tell you that they *"instinctively know."* This type is the discernment that we need to be operating in daily. Practical discernment is not the gift of discerning of spirits, which is something we will cover in the next chapter.

Practical discernment is for every single believer. What one can obtain in the spirit, so can another. We have the same opportunity of intimacy with the Father that makes the atmosphere ripe within our spirit to receive all the Bible says we can have. The degree one can operate in discernment is the degree they have been practicing. Practical discernment is for every single believer at every individual level of faith. It doesn't matter if you are recently saved or have been serving the Lord for 40 years or more. It is yours if you want it, and if you are ready to work at it. In the coming chapters, we will discuss ways to train your discernment.

Roberts Lairdon writes in his book Sharpen Your Discernment:

> *"When you see someone who operates strongly in discernment, it's not an unusual gift given to a special person. It's not something for you to "ooh" and "aah" over. What you're seeing is someone who has developed the discernment equipment that we've all been given. Instead of putting that person on a pedestal, let them inspire you to begin developing what you've been given."*[1]

What Discernment is Not

Discernment is not, I repeat **IS NOT**, an opportunity for gossip, fault finding, or criticism. There is no room in discernment for assumptions or presumptions. The only things you should know for sure is that you know absolutely nothing and are trusting God to reveal all you need to know. God did not give us discernment so we could destroy the character of another person. Do not get on your phone and blab everything you picked up in the spirit about anyone or any ministry. Pray for that person or ministry instead. It is a dangerous thing to come after a minister or ministry based on your discernment. God is very clear on this matter. It is written in 1 Chronicles 16:22 and Psalm 105:15 not to touch God's anointed ones or bring harm to His prophets. Steer clear of using your discernment to bring harm to anyone. But instead heed what Galatians 6:1 says, *"Brothers and sisters, if someone is caught doing something wrong, you who are directed by the Ruach (God's Spirit), restore such a person in a spirit of gentleness—looking closely at yourself, so you are not tempted also."*

Discernment is not a chance for you to pass judgment upon someone or inflict condemnation. Doing this not only causes our gift to become a tool in the hands of the enemy to strike down another but we will also damage ourselves. Pray about what you see and only share with those you trust who will help you pray about what you have seen or felt. I have come to know that when the Lord shows me something about someone or a ministry, it is His call for me to intercede on their behalf not spread the information around. The more we are faithful to do this, the more He will trust us with what He is revealing.

Discernment is not child's play. It is the mark of a mature Christian and a faithful follower of Christ. Hebrews 5:14 states, *"But solid food is for the mature, who through practice have their senses trained to discern both good and evil."* It is not a game to be played at parties.

Discernment is not meant to bring fear but freedom. It is easy to do with all the teachings on witchcraft out there to get caught up in thinking that there are boogie men behind every bush. When we are shown things in the spirit realm, it is an opportunity to trust the Father and His goodness. Do not let fear guide your discernment. Seeing the enemy can be overpowering at times. Remember, what you focus on is what you will experience. Discernment was not given to believers for us to become paranoid about every little thing. The Word tells us 365 times to fear not. Fear will corrupt your discernment, causing a misfiring of the communication center between your spirit and the Spirit of the Lord. When this happens, it will cause us to mistake the enemy's presence for God's and vice versa. I have witnessed this happen in people.

Discernment is not for the prideful. I have said this before, but I cannot repeat it enough - pride has no place in discernment. Yes, it is very easy to do, especially if you are rapidly developing and you feel others are not as far along as you are. Pride will cause you to fall (Prov. 16:18). Pride will make you critical of others and give an open door for the enemy to come and wreak havoc on you. You must always remove yourself (preconceived ideas, emotions, and agendas) out of the equation when it comes to discernment. James 4:7 says, *"Therefore submit to God. But resist the devil, and he will flee from you."* Always submit yourself, and your discernment to God and pride will not have an in road.

One good place to start with discernment is to ask the Father to cleanse your natural senses and realign them to His purposes. Repent of what you need to repent of, renounce what you need to renounce, break off what needs to be broken off, and then speak the Word of God over yourself to bless your spirit. It all begins with submission to the Father and His will. If you have found yourself being prideful, judgmental and critical of others because of the level of your discernment or tried to shut down your discernment due to fear, please take some time to repent of those things right now so that you can be all you are called to be.

This prayer by Kevin Stevens is a great place to start for activating your discernment:

"LORD, I pray right now in the Name of Jesus that you would anoint my eyes with eye salve that I may see.

LORD, I don't just want to see in the natural, but LORD, activate my spiritual eyes to see what is taking place in the realm of the spirit.

LORD, help me to know, in every situation, You have sent your Spirit and your angels to protect me from the enemy and even to bring heavenly provision when needed.

LORD, I also ask you to open my ears to attune them to Your voice. I want to hear Your voice above everything else.

LORD, sharpen my spiritual senses this day. LORD, open my eyes to the seer dimension! In Jesus' Name!"[2]

Chapter Two
Discernment or the Gift of Discerning of Spirits?

*"But to each one is given the manifestation of the Spirit for the profit of all. For to one is given through the Spirit the word of wisdom, and to another the word of knowledge, according to the same Spirit; to another faith, by the same Spirit; and to another gifts of healings, by the one Spirit; and to another workings of miracles; and to another prophecy; and to another **discernings of spirits**; to another different kinds of tongues; and to another the interpretation of tongues. But the one and the same Spirit works all of these, distributing to each one separately as he desires."*

-- 1 Corinthians 12:7-11 NHE (emphasis is mine)

I have been taught and heard it taught for years that the gift of discernment is only for a certain few. And, that not every believer has discernment. This teaching is incorrect. Discernment is for every single believer no matter their maturity level. It is highly essential to note there is a difference between practical discernment, which each believer has by default and the gift of discerning of spirits. Every believer can discern to a certain degree. The gift of discerning of spirits comes by asking for and seeking after it. It is a gift of the Holy Spirit. The line between the two frequently gets blurred due to how the two are so intertwined.

C. Peter Wagner, in his book, Discover Your Spiritual Gifts, writes, *"discerning of spirits is defined as the special ability to know with assurance whether certain behaviors purported to be of God are in reality divine, human or satanic".*[1]

The difference between discernment and the gift of discerning of spirits is discernment is a

6

natural ability while the gift of discerning of spirits is a gift of the Holy Spirit as you see in the above scripture. On his blog, Pedro Anosike writes the following about the difference between practical discernment and the gift of discernment, *"The difference between the gift of discerning spirits and having discernment is like the distance between continents. Majorly, it does not just deal with the mental realm and its motive but detects the kind of spirit in operation. It bypasses whether the motive is good or bad".[2]*

It is within the confines of the gift of discerning of spirits that intercession, warfare, and practical discernment collide. When God reveals to us what spirit is in operation, where ever we are, it is for us to begin to intercede as to prevent an evil spirit from working and influencing the people. The gift of discerning of spirits does not just refer to discerning the spiritual state of other people – it also refers to discerning the spiritual state of ourselves. We have to discern ourselves always to ensure we are in alignment with the heart of the Father.

Both the gift of discernment and practical discernment operate by our five senses. The gift of discernment will affect us more profoundly than in practical discernment. This type is what Paul Cox refers to as *"Sensory Discernment."* He goes into more detail on his website, Aslan's Place.[3]

To better help explain the use of our senses in discernment, we only need to look to scripture to see how they operate.

Manifestations of the Senses in Discernment: *More on this in Chapter Four.*

➢ **Touch:** Acts 12:7, I Kings 19:7; Mark 9:17-20

➢ **Smell:** 2 Corinthians 2:15-16; Revelation 5 & 8

➢ **Taste:** Ezekiel 3:1-3, Revelation 10:8-10

➢ **Sight:** Genesis 18:1-2, Exodus 3:2, Isaiah 6:1-2, Luke 10:18, Revelation 13

➢ **Hearing:** Genesis 3:8 & 12:1, Exodus 19:19, Joshua 1:1, 1 Samuel 3:4, Gospels of Matthew, Mark, Luke, & John, Revelation

Can every believer operate in the gift of discerning of spirits? I believe so. It is a spiritual gift given by the Holy Spirit to edify the Saints. If you want it, ask for it. According to 1 Corinthians 12:31 (HNV), Paul writes, *"But earnestly desire the best gifts. Moreover, I show a more excellent way to you."* The word for *"desire"* is the Greek word *"zēloō,"* which means to *"burn with zeal, be zealous in the pursuit of good."* James writes this in James 1:5 (NIV), *"If any of you lacks wisdom, you should ask God, who gives generously to all without finding fault, and it will be given to you."*

We read in Acts 10:34, *"Then Peter opened his mouth and said, 'I truly understand that God is not one to show favoritism."* God shows no partiality to anyone (Gal. 2:6). Ask Him and believe in faith that you receive. Not only this, but as co-heirs with Christ (Romans 8:17), the same Spirit that rested on Yeshua is available to us. All we have to do is ask for it to be activated. I have heard it said that to the degree you are submitted to God is the depth you will be able to operate in the gifts of the Spirit. The same is true for the discernment.

I firmly believe that both practical discernment and the gift of discernment will flow together, empowering each other the more we operate in both. For me, it is hard to distinguish where one begins and the other ends with my discernment. I have developed in both. Are there people who are more trained and operate better in both than me? Absolutely. I fully intend on getting to that level and beyond for the glory of the One who gave me this gift.

If you genuinely desire the gift of discerning of spirits, then pray this prayer in faith and believe:

Heavenly Father,

I ask in the name of Your Son, Yeshua, to receive the Gift of Discerning of Spirits. Your Word says to earnestly seek the gifts, so I set my face like flint to seek the gifts the Holy Spirit has for me as Your child. I ask in faith to receive the gift of discerning of spirits. Allow me to see clearly through the spiritual realm so

8

that I may be an effective intercessor and warrior for Christ. Teach me to partner with the Holy Spirit so that I may walk in the gift of discerning of spirits. Grant me understanding and wisdom to appropriately process and release what You are showing me. I pray these things in the name of your Son Yeshua. Amen.

Chapter Three
What is Discernment For?

Both practical discernment and the gift of discernment, have distinct purposes in the lives of believers. Each purpose develops us in a specific area of our walk with God. I have listed out a few of those areas. This list is in no way exhaustive.

Discernment Allows Us to Become Better Watchmen and Intercessors.

It is like the difference of seeing with our natural eyes and seeing with a pair of binoculars. We can only see so far, relying only on our natural eyes. With binoculars, we can see far beyond what the naked eye can see. Relying solely on our senses in discernment is just like staring across a vast field with just our eyes. We can vaguely see what is there, but not in great detail. We can only know in part. When we cross over into spiritual discernment, the spiritual world around us becomes more apparent. And we gain a better understanding of how and when to pray.

Think of it this way. We cannot know for sure if someone is hiding behind a wall; however, with thermal imaging, you can see a person's heat signature. Our natural senses can cause us to jump to conclusions and assume there is no one behind the wall. Using the right equipment, one can see behind the wall and determine the gender, height, weight of the person behind the wall as well as if they are carrying a weapon or not.

The same goes for discernment. Always use natural senses first. What do your eyes behold? What is the environment telling you about the possible spiritual condition of an area or person? Examples would be dead trees, dead patches of grass, behavioral patterns of wildlife, strange smells, etc. Do not give into paranoia here. Learn about nature so you will not make rash

10

judgments based solely on natural observations. Sometimes a flock of birds is just a flock of birds. After looking at the natural, look through the spirit, and see what is behind the physical. The natural realm will always reflect what is going on in the spiritual realm. The two are that closely connected.

Discernment is a Defensive Weapon of Warfare.

If we use discernment correctly, it can and will save us from making erroneous decisions that have the possibility of evil lurking behind them. How can discernment save us? The answer is found in 1 John 4:1, *"Beloved, believe not every spirit, but try the spirits whether they are of God: because many false prophets are gone out into the world."*

This goes back to what I mentioned about Chuck Pierce's teaching about discerning daily. He goes on to say that we must discern daily by the Word and by the Spirit.[1] But, what does that mean? All of our discernment should be first and foremost grounded in the Word of God and the intimacy of the Holy Spirit. If we cannot base our discernment off scripture, then we are in error.

We are commanded to examine any spiritual teaching with our critical faculties to see whether the presenter is handling the Word of God accurately. Because evil spirits can produce paranormal phenomena, the scripture exhorts us to prove or test the spirits, holding fast to what is good according to 1 Thessalonians 5:21. The Holy Spirit will always bring to our remembrance the Word of God (John 14:26) to help us discern.

I love how John Ramirez puts it. He writes, *"We need to discern and be prepared and quick on our spiritual feet, so that we can overcome any adversity or any fiery dart of the enemy."*[2] When we are aware of the operation of the enemy and the forces of darkness, we can appropriately pray against them. Discernment will give us insight into how to pray and battle in the Spirit. It is also a shield. Proverbs 2:11 states, *"Discretion will watch over you —*

11

discernment will guard you (emphasis mine).

Discernment and Prophesy Go Hand in Hand.

Acts 13:9-12 gives us the account of Elymas the sorcerer's encounter with Paul, *"But Saul, who was also called Paul, was filled with the Holy Spirit. He looked straight at Elymas and said, 'You son of the devil! You are an enemy of everything that is right! You are full of evil tricks and lies, always trying to change the Lord's truths into lies. Now the Lord will touch you, and you will be blind. For a time, you will not be able to see anything—not even the light from the sun.' Then everything became dark for Elymas, and he walked around, trying to find someone to lead him by the hand."*

It is imperative to note here that discernment is not the seer (prophet) gift. A seer is, as defined by Dictionary.com, is one who is *"able, through supernatural insight, to see what the future holds."* The seer gift is a prophetic gifting. The focus of these two gifts is different. Discernment focuses on the source of something while the seer gift focuses on seeing into the spirit realm and declaring what one sees the Lord is doing. These two gifts are separate. You can argue with Paul if you like as he separates the two gifts in 1 Corinthians 12:7-11. That is not to say, however, that someone who is a strong discerner cannot operate in the seer gift. The two gifts work in tandem with each other. Christian author David Backus writes on his blog, The Free Believers Network, *"I like to call the gift of discernment the twin gift of prophecy. People who are prophets or who work closely with prophets possess this gift as well. It complements and tempers the prophetic gift nicely."*[3]

It is by the spirit of prophecy that one receives a word of knowledge, but it takes discernment to know who that word was for. The two gifts need each other. They function hand in hand with one another. Helen Calder writes about this on her blog:

"Someone who operates in the seer gift of prophetic ministry needs discernment,

12

to help weigh up whether or not a vision, encounter or visionary experience is of the Holy Spirit. Likewise, someone who has a gift of discernment needs the encouragement and perspective that the prophetic ministry and gift brings. When we perceive the enemy at work, for example, the prophetic gift sees past what is currently going on, to God's intended outcome. And that is a game-changer!"[4]

Discernment is Revelatory.

The Spirit of the Lord that dwells in you will help you, through discernment, by either bearing witness to or against the spirit in operation in another. He will also give you the knowledge of how to pray concerning what is being taught, and prove prophetic words which have been spoken over you. It will also help you in knowing the voice of the Father. Discernment will also reveal to you the trauma that occurred in a location. Most people operate at this level of discernment without even realizing it. They dismiss what they are *"picking up"* on in the spirit as a prophetic inclination when this is instead discernment bringing revelation. Discernment will also allow us to know whether we are having a divine encounter with the Lord Himself, an angel or a demonic presence. Our discernment will also help us determine what type of angel or demon we are encountering. This revelatory discernment will also help you in finding gates and doors (portals) in the spirit realm, which are affecting the atmosphere and help in distinguishing between Godly and demonic openings.

In 2018, I attended a discernment conference in Alabama. While there, my back began to heat up as if I were in front of a fire. The gentleman leading the conference said an archangel had walked in the room to deliver a message to us. Ever since then, I can quickly identify when an archangel comes into a place. I know a wonderful woman of God who senses the Seraphim by a pressure that happens on a specific spot on her head. These are all revelations this lady, and I have come to have concerning various forms of angels using our discernment. As you grow in your discernment, the Lord will grant you revelation as to what you are sensing. All you have to do is have faith in Him and listen to His voice.

In the natural, we know when someone is seated next to us and when someone enters the room. We can feel the temperature change as we get close to someone. We can hear their breathing. Smell their cologne. Hear the sound of their clothing as they move. We know that someone is there even when we do not see them. This is part of our discernment. Remember, discernment takes practice and to give yourself grace as you grow. You will not be able to operate in all areas at once.

Practical Application 1:

This is a very easy and fun exercise to do with a friend. All you are doing is stretching yourself to be able to sense another person in the room.

➢ Sit quietly alone in a room with your eyes closed.

➢ Have your buddy walk into the room as stealthily as possible. Can you sense their presence when they enter?

➢ Have them move about the room and see if you can determine where they are.

➢ Take turns with this exercise as often as you can to help grow you.

➢ **CHALLENGE:** Try this exercise again with distractions like the radio or TV being on. Take notes on how you discernment changed with distractions in the room.

Practical Application 2:

Here is another fun sensory exercise to do in a small group. You will need to turn on some worship music for background noise. You will also need to ask one of your friends to be an observer. So grab a few friends and give this a try.

➢ Have everyone else form a close circle in the center of the room, and close their eyes.

➢ Walk around the outside of the circle as quietly as possible without touching anyone. And stop behind someone.

➢ Have your observer ask those in the circle to raise their hands when they think someone is behind them.

➢ Let everyone take turns being the observer as well as the one walking around the circle.

Practical Application 3:

Here is an easy exercise you can do in the comfort of your own home. You will need to turn off all the distractions (i.e., electronic devices, TV, computer, radio, etc.) before doing this. You will need some quietness and stillness to be able to sense as you begin to train yourself. You are only after being able to know that you are in the presence of something. Grab your discernment journal and give this a try.

➢ Cover yourself in prayer and worship. Always start here for every exercise we will do.

➢ Sit quietly and ask the Father to allow you to sense your angels.

➢ Ask the Father to send each type of angel so you can sense the difference and take notes on how your body reacts to each one.

➢ Ask to feel the presence of Yeshua and take note of how your body reacts.

➢ Praise and thank the Father for allowing you to experience these things.

➢ Do not be upset if you feel absolutely nothing the first time you try this or even the next few times. It is a process.

➤ **CHALLENGE:** Try again this time with distractions (i.e., electronic devices, TV, computer, radio, etc.). Take notes on how your discernment changes with distractions in the room.

Practical Application 4:

Try this exercise in a safe space such as a ministry building or church. I do not recommend doing this at your home just yet. Make sure you have no distractions.

➤ Cover yourself in prayer and worship. Always start here for every exercise we will do.

➤ Ask the Father to cover you in the Blood of Yeshua and shut down any open door in your bloodline before moving to the next step of this exercise.

➤ Sit quietly and ask the Father to allow you to feel a demonic presence.

➤ Do not get in fear here. Just relax and know that you are covered in the Blood.

➤ Take note of how your body reacts.

➤ Ask Jesus to remove the entity from your presence.

➤ Praise the Lord for the experience and knowledge gained from the experience.

➤ **CHALLENGE:** When you are more comfortable, repeat this exercise with distractions. Remember to take notes on how having distractions change your ability to discern.

Chapter Four
Sensory Involvement in Discernment

Hebrews 5:14 states (TLV), *"But solid food is for the mature, who through practice have their senses trained to discern both good and evil."* Our sensory perception was created by God to help us in discernment. As you mature in your discernment, your senses will come into alignment and operate to help guide you. What does it look like to have our senses trained? How can we arrive at a place where our sensory perception operates to our benefit and to that of the Kingdom? Through practice. The more we practice, the more comfortable we will become in using our senses in discernment.

Scientists have discovered that we have a total of 12 senses. We have the senses of touch, of life, of movement, and of balance which relates to our body. The senses of smell, taste, sight, and temperature are how we perceive the physical world around us. The senses of hearing, speech, thought, and ego relates to the immaterial or spiritual world. In this chapter, we will look at five of the 12 senses – touch, taste, smell, sight, and hearing.

What we do not realize is our spirits can perceive through its senses that which will affect our natural senses. We are triune beings consisting of a spirit, a soul, and a body. All three function together to make us one person. There is only a very thin layer between the spirit and natural worlds. We are as far away from the spirit realm as our next breath. We must keep this in mind when our senses come into line with our discernment.

Our senses have a direct impact on our emotions. Take trauma for an example. It can be triggered by sounds, sights, taste, smells, and specific touches. My husband doesn't like coffee due to a traumatic experience as a young child from a prank that his older sister pulled on him. She told him it was the most delicious cup of hot chocolate ever. He took a sip believing her only to discover a very bitter cup of coffee. The taste of the coffee and even its smell are tied to that traumatic experience as a child.

Certain sounds and visuals can put us on edge. Think about horror movies. The tone of the music mixed with the imagery will increase our flight or fight reflexes. Romantic images mixed with soft, romantic music create feelings of love and euphoria. Nature sounds relax us and lower blood pressure.

There may have been times when our ancestors traded the senses to the enemy for power and money. A bloodline curse then comes over our sensory perception preventing us from operating fully in discernment. This curse will need to be broken off before your senses will completely come alive in discernment. Inner healing and deliverance are amazing tools for releasing freedom in your senses. If you have never consecrated and dedicated your senses to the Lord, you may want to do that. Ask the Holy Spirit for the verbiage to use when you pray and be obedient to pray what you receive.

The Sense of Touch

The sense of touch is a very complex sense. It consists of two parts – discriminative and emotional. The discriminative touch system gives us the facts about our environment, such as physical pain, location, movement, and the strength of touch. Our emotional touch system is a much slower delivery system. This part of our touch sense helps us distinguish between the touch of friends, family, and lovers. It is crucial to social bonding. Emotions can also be tied to the sense of touch.

So let's take this into the spirit realm. Can we physically feel something in the spirit realm? Yes. I know it is a hard concept to wrap your head around. How can someone touch something in the spirit realm and yet experience it in the natural considering there is no physical form in the spirit? If you think of your body like a glove for your spirit, it begins to make sense. In the natural, when you have a glove on your hand, you can still feel through the glove. Our spirit is the same way. It feels through our physical senses.

Let's look at a few scriptures to help put this into perspective. Isaiah had an angel touch his lips with the coal from the altar before the throne of God in Isaiah 6:7. Acts 12:7 says, *"Suddenly an angel of the Lord appeared, and a light shone in the cell. He poked Peter on the side and woke him up, saying, 'Get up! Quick!' And the chains fell off his hands."* An angel, which is a spirit, touched Peter's spirit manifesting in the natural sense of being touched. This same thing happens to Elijah in 1 Kings 19:7.

Even demons can affect our sense of touch and bring physical harm at times. From the spirit realm, both angels and demons can physically touch us. We need to know what each touch feels like so we can distinguish good from evil. Do not take this as permission to go chasing down demons so you can know how each feel. *NEVER, NEVER, EVER* go demon chasing! Concentrate on getting to know how the touch of the Holy Spirit and the angels feel. Then when something not of God touches you, you will immediately recognize the difference.

Practical Application 1:

You will be feeling something from the spirit realm. You will be using your hands for this. So get ready for a new experience. Remember to remove all distractions before beginning. For some of you, this will be different than any other experience you have had with discernment. So take a deep breath and relax.

➢ Cover yourself in worship and prayer. Always start here for every exercise we will do.

➢ Ask the Father to allow you to physically touch one of your angels or have them touch you.

➢ Reach out your non-dominant hand (if you are right-handed, this will be your left hand and vice versa) as if to touch something. You may find it easier to do this with your eyes closed.

➢ Note your sensations so you can remember.

➢ What does it feel like?

➢ Is there form to what you are touching? Is it hard or soft? Squishy or solid?

➢ Does the angel feel warm, or is it cold?

➢ Does your hand tingle? Or do you experience pressure on your hand?

➢ What emotions come up as you touch the angels?

➢ Repeat until you are very familiar with what the Godly angelic feels like.

➢ **CHALLENGE:** Repeat this exercise with distractions. Remember to take notes on how having distractions change your ability to discern.

Practical Application 2:

This application is a very safe exercise to do from the comfort of your home. Remember to remove all distractions before beginning and relax. The more relaxed and comfortable you are, the easier it is to feel what your spirit is feeling physically. I suggest using your non-dominant hand again for this exercise.

➢ Cover yourself in prayer and worship. Always start here for every exercise we will do.

➢ Ask the Father to cover you in the Blood of Yeshua and shut down any open door in your bloodline before moving to the next step of this exercise.

➢ Ask the Father to allow you to physically touch a spiritual door (portal) and take notes of how your body reacts.

➢ Is there a form to what you are touching? Is it hard or soft? Rough or smooth? Squishy or solid?

➢ Is it warm, or is it cold?

➢ Does your hand tingle?

➢ What emotions arise?

➢ Ask Yeshua to close and remove the door from your presence.

➢ Praise the Lord for the experience and knowledge gained from it.

➢ **CHALLENGE:** Repeat this exercise with distractions. Remember to take notes on how having distractions change your ability to discern.

The Sense of Smell

You can smell food cooking, and it tastes as good as it smells. Why? Because our sense of smell has enhanced our sense of taste. Even when we think we are tasting, we are in reality smelling. These two senses work in tandem with each other. But, we will discuss taste in a moment.

Our noses can pick up on countless fragrances and varying combinations of aromas. 80% of the times we experience taste through the sense of smell. We are continually using our sense of smell, even when we are unaware. Fragrances will also come with emotions. The scent of baking bread in the oven, for example, may bring to mind fond memories of visits to your grandmother's house and how she always made you feel loved.

The sense of smell comes into play with our discernment as we can pick up on the aroma of Christ, God, the angels, death, as well as a wide variety of demonic entities. Did you ever think that Christ has a fragrance? Ephesians 5:2 tells us about the fragrance of Christ, *"...gave Himself up for us as an offering and sacrifice to God for a fragrant aroma."* Many, many times, I have been in prayerful worship and smelled the amazing aroma of God. There are no words to describe it. It is something that has to be experienced. Every believer should experience the fragrance of God.

We have a fragrance in the spirit realm as we are co-heirs with Christ. 2 Corinthians 2:15-16 says, *"For we are the **aroma** of Messiah to God, among those who are being saved and those who are perishing— to the one an **aroma** from death to death, to the other an **aroma** from life to life. Who is competent for these things?"* (emphasis mine). We smell more and more like Him in the spirit realm as we become more like Him. In both the fifth and eighth chapters of Revelation, it speaks of the saints' prayers being incense and mixed with incense in heaven before the Throne of God. Our prayers have a spiritual fragrance.

The demonic has a very distinctive odor. I have been on prayer assignments and smelled the strong stench of sulfur and ash. This is the scent of a high-level demonic general. Other times I have experienced what can only be described as the foul odor of cat urine. I have smelled the demonic on a person as well. Sometimes unclean spirits will smell like human dung. You may smell them long before you can sense them any other way. These are odors that you will not forget.

Practical Application 3:

This application will be one of the most exciting parts of our exercises - to smell the fragrance of God and the angels. It may take a bit of practice before you can fully distinguish the smell of God. Just be patient.

- ➢ Enter into a time of worshipful prayer.
- ➢ Ask the Father to let you smell Him, Jesus, the Holy Spirit, and the angels. These will be different from each other. Ask the Father what you smell like in the spirit.
- ➢ Ask the Father to let you experience the fragrance of the prayers of the saints and your prayers.
- ➢ Take note of each fragrance and what emotion they evoke in you.
- ➢ **CHALLENGE:** Repeat this exercise with distractions. Remember to take notes on how having distractions change your ability to discern.

Practical Application 4:

This part will not be fun but necessary to have a full scope of how your sense of smell can help you in discernment. This time we will ask to experience the scent of the demonic. I ask that you do this exercise in a very safe environment such as a church or ministry building or outdoors away from your personal property. If you are uncomfortable doing this alone, have a trusted prayer warrior with you.

➢ Cover yourself in prayer and worship. Always start here for every exercise we will do.

➢ Ask the Father to cover you in the Blood of Yeshua and shut down any open door.

➢ Sit quietly and ask the Father to allow you to smell an unclean spirit.

➢ Ask to smell a demon. Do not get in fear here. Relax and know that you are protected.

➢ Take note of how your body reacts.

➢ What emotions come up?

➢ What does the smell remind you of? Do your best to describe it.

➢ How does the smell differ from each other? How are they similar?

➢ Ask Jesus to remove the entity or entities from your presence.

➢ Ask Jesus to close and remove the door from your presence.

➢ Praise the Lord for the experience and knowledge gained from it.

➢ **CHALLENGE:** Repeat this exercise with distractions. Remember to take notes on how having distractions change your ability to discern.

The Sense of Taste

We think we know this sense, but do we? We view taste as to how food and drink affect our tastebuds on our tongue. We have also heard taste referred to as someone's personal preferences in style and design. This description of *"taste"* is not correct, and is a preference not the actual sense of taste. But this does not appropriately define the sense of taste.

Our tongues contain receptors known as taste buds. The taste buds send signals to our brains, allowing us to perceive taste. Food will cause our brains to give off a signal in these categories: salty, bitter, sweet, sour, and *"Unami,"* which means savory and pleasant. And yet, there are no receptors that signal a metallic taste in our mouths. But, we get that from time to time. No one seems to be able to explain why. There is another element of our natural sense of taste called *"Kokumi."* This term is used to describe richness, heartiness, and thickness of flavors. When we refer to the flavor of something, three senses are actually involved: taste, touch, and smell. These three senses combine to help us experience the depth of a flavor. This combination is what I believe happens as we taste in the spirit. The senses of taste, touch, and smell combine to give us depth in the spirit realm so that we can *"taste and see that the Lord is good"* (Psalm 34:9).

Ezekiel experienced a taste in the spirit as seen in the Ezekiel 3:3, *"as He said to me, "Son of man, feed your belly with this scroll that I am giving you and fill your stomach with it." I ate it, and it tasted as sweet as honey."* Ezekiel didn't physically eat a scroll. This experience was a manifestation of the spirit realm.

Again, we see a similar occurrence happening to the Apostle John in Revelation 10:9-10, *"So I went to the angel, telling him to give me the little scroll. And he tells me, 'Take and eat it. It will be bitter to your stomach, but sweet as honey in your mouth.' So I took the little scroll from the angel's hand and ate it. It was sweet as honey in my mouth; but when I had swallowed it, my stomach was made bitter."*

Death has a taste. Hebrews 2:9 says, *"But we see One who was made for a little while lower than the angels—namely, Yeshua. He is now crowned with glory and honor, because of the death He suffered so that, by the grace of God, He might **taste** death for everyone."* (Emphasis mine.) As you see, taste plays an essential role in our discernment as well as the prophetic.

Practical Application 5:

This exercise may be challenging as you are training your senses. But, do not back down. The Lord will help you through this like all of the rest of the exercises thus far. Just remember to keep trying if you do not experience it the first time.

- ➢ Remove all distractions
- ➢ Enter into a time of worshipful prayer.
- ➢ Ask the Father to let you taste the manna of heaven, something sweet and then something bitter.
- ➢ Take note of each one tastes and what emotion they evoke in you.
- ➢ **CHALLENGE:** Repeat this exercise with distractions. Remember to take notes on how having distractions change your ability to discern.

The Sense of Sight

Our eyes are one of the most important sensory organs we possess. It is said that the sense of sight is the most difficult sense to go without. The enemy would love nothing more than to block your visual discernment. Vision occurs when light is processed by the eye and then interpreted by the brain. Light passes through the cornea. The amount of that light received is based on the opening of our iris. It will open wide when things are dimly lit and shrink in bright light. Light passes through the lens of our eye and then focused onto the retina. From there, the retina converts that light into a nerve impulse that travels to the brain where the information is then processed into an image. Close to 80% of our sensory perception is received through our eyes. We make a fraction of a second decision based on what we see.

The majority of people can perceive close to 150 colors. These colors affect our moods. Blues and greens make us more relaxed while red colors cause us to become more agitated and has been proven to make us overeat. Yellows and oranges can make people feel happy. Gray can make us feel sad or depressed.

There is an old saying that says, *"the eyes are the windows to the soul."* This quote from Smart Vision Labs' website echoes this, *"The eyes are the physical portal through which data from your environment is collected and sent to your brain for processing."*[1] Did you catch that? The eyes are a *"physical portal."* Maybe that is why visual stimulation can severely alter our psyche, wreak havoc on our emotions, or bring us to a place of euphoria. Most mind-control programming occurs through visual and auditory stimuli.

Matthew 6:22-23 says, *"The eye is the lamp of the body. Therefore if your eye is good, your whole body will be full of light. But if your eye is bad, your body will be full of darkness. If therefore, the light that is in you is darkness, how great is the darkness!"*

The enemy knows that vision is tied to our direction in life. If he can blind us spiritually or contaminate our sight, then he can gain the upper hand very quickly over us. This happens more readily to men than to women. Men respond more readily to visual stimuli than women do. That is why it is so easy for the enemy to capture men with pornography.

Our eyes can see into the spirit realm and appropriately interpret what we perceive visually. Often, we associate seeing in the spirit to the prophetic. The Bible is full of examples of people seeing into the spirit realm and receiving revelation as to what they saw. All are prime examples of the seer gift and discernment merging to bring clear revelation. Without discernment, these prophets would not have been able to grasp what God who was showing and explaining. We too must allow our discernment to merge with the prophetic to bring the

Kingdom of God to Earth.

Isaiah saw, in the spirit realm, the Lord upon His throne and the angels that fly around the throne (Isaiah 6:1-2). Ezekiel witnessed abominations in the temple (Ezekiel 8) and saw the measurements of a new temple all in the spirit realm (Ezekiel 40). Jeremiah saw an almond tree in the spirit and a boiling pot (Jeremiah 1:11-19). Amos saw a plumb line (Amos 7:8). The Book of Revelation is full of examples of John seeing into the spirit realm.

What can we see in the spirit realm? Matthew 5:8 states, *"Blessed are the pure in heart, for they shall see God."* The word for *"see"* here is the Greek word *"horaō"* which means *"to see with the eyes; to see with the mind, to perceive, know; to stare at; to discern clearly (physically or mentally)."* This verse tells us we can see God. I have seen angels around people and in church services, and I have seen Jesus walking the aisle in church services. I have also seen demons sitting on people's backs. I have seen the demonic manifest as slightly transparent animals. I have seen angels appear as balls of light. I have seen spiritual gates and doors/portals. A word of warning here, if you please. Once you begin to be able to see into the spirit realm, things will start to manifest. The majority of the time, these things were already there. You are just seeing them for the first time. Do not be alarmed. This is normal. You will learn how to filter what is your battle and what needs to be left alone as your discernment grows.

In this exercise, you will be asking to see and discern in the spirit realm visually. This will be difficult for some, while others will be able to immediately. Do not fret if you do not see at first. Just relax and take it slow.

➢ Remove all distractions, and enter into a time of worshipful prayer.

➢ Ask the Father to let you see what your angels look like. Take note of what you see. Can you see color? How tall are they? Are they carrying weapons? Can you make out facial features?

➢ Ask if you can see the altar that is before the Throne of God. Make sure to take notes.

➢ Always remember to praise God for your experience.

➢ **CHALLENGE:** Repeat this exercise with distractions. Remember to take notes on how having distractions change your ability to discern.

The Sense of Hearing

Our sense of hearing is quite impressive when you look at it. Our ears are made up of six parts – the pinna or auricle, the ear canal, the eardrum, the ossicles which consist of the hammer, anvil and stirrup, the cochlea, and the auditory nerve. All of these tiny parts working together to capture sound waves and convert them to electrical pulses to our brain to be interpreted as sound.

The pinna (the outer ear flap) acts as a trap to catch sound waves and channel them into the ear canal. Those waves hit the eardrum and cause the bones in the middle ear to vibrate. The cochlea is filled with a liquid and lined with tiny hair cells. We are born with about 12,000 of these hair cells. Sound waves cause the fluid to vibrate. These tiny hair cells convert the vibrations into electric signals that are picked up by the auditory nerve and shipped off to the brain to be interpreted as sound. This process happens within millions of a second.

Hearing in the spirit is not as easy as it seems. In this modern age, we are constantly bombarded with sounds from every angle. From construction zones or church services, we are continually hearing. Some of these sounds or noises can overload us and make us want to hide in a quiet place. At times, we are so surrounded by sound, and it can drown out the voice of God in our lives.

What we hear coming from the spirit realm may not always make sense. It could be the sound of random voices in a distance, drums, bells, chimes, an alarm with no one or anything else around us. We hear things and wonder if we are going crazy. I have been all alone in my house and heard a man's voice ask me a question, and I immediately knew it was not the voice of God.

Anything that produces sound in the spirit can be heard; this includes God, angels, demons, the four living creatures, the elders around the Throne. Even the cloud of witnesses can be heard. We can hear God's voice as Abram did in Genesis 12:1 and Joshua in Joshua 1:1, and young Samuel in 1 Samuel 3:4. Throughout the Four Gospels and into Revelation, we see many Biblical examples of hearing in the spirit realm. In Genesis 3:8, we read about Adam and Eve hearing God's sound as He walked through the Garden of Eden. God's sound...what would that be like for us to hear and recognize the God of all creation as He moved?

Every living thing has been scientifically proven to give off a sound. Even the planets and stars in the heavens themselves produce sound. We create a sound in the spirit realm as we are spirit beings. I have heard teaching about money, which is a physical object, speaks either for or against us in the Courts of Heaven, which is in the spirit realm. To be able to hear clearly in the spirit will take practice and patience. You will have to trust what you hear when you hear it. The more you attune yourself to the voice of God and the voice of the Holy Spirit, the more you will readily be able to know when the enemy is speaking to you as opposed to the Father. Seek after the voice of the Father first! Jesus told us in John 10:27, *"My sheep hear My voice. I know them, and they follow Me."* Become intimately familiar with His voice, and everything else will fall into place.

Practical Application 7:

You will need ample time for this exercise. Be sure you can carve out enough time every day to devote to developing your hearing discernment. Make sure you do not allow any distractions as you train.

- ➢ Enter into intimate worship and prayer.
- ➢ Allow yourself to become quiet in spirit, soul and body.
- ➢ Be mindful of your own thoughts, and do not let your mind wander.
- ➢ Ask the Father to be able to hear what sound you personally make in the spirit realm.
- ➢ Ask to hear what He sounds like when He moves.
- ➢ Ask to hear His voice clearly.
- ➢ Ask to hear the voice of your angel(s).
- ➢ Take notes as to how each sound makes you feel emotionally.
- ➢ **CHALLENGE:** Repeat this exercise with distractions. Remember to take notes on how having distractions change your ability to discern.

Chapter Five
Personal and Group Discernment

We are called to discern daily. This practice includes discerning ourselves, our own homes and businesses regularly, discerning others and other places, as well as discerning who and what we allow into our lives. We need to operate in a level of discernment that comes as naturally as breathing to us. It will help us grow in Christ and help to stretch our discernment. The more we press in, the more the Father reveals to us what we need to deal with. It all begins with discerning our selves.

Personal Discernment

When discerning yourself, you must be careful not to jump to conclusions. Just because we think we have already dealt with an issue doesn't mean there isn't a deeper level of cleansing and healing we need to do. We cannot allow what we already know about ourselves or what someone has told us to cloud our discernment. The Lord wants each of us healed and delivered so we can help others. Before we can help anyone, we have to be clean ourselves. One of the best ways to begin with inner healing is what I call personal discernment or self discernment. Self discernment is a discipline and must be practiced regularly. Just like regular physical check-ups, regular spiritual check-ups will help us stay on top of our game.

Matthew 7:3-5 says, *"Why do you look at the speck in your brother's eye, but do not notice the beam in your own eye? Or how will you say to your brother, 'Let me take the speck out of your eye,' and look, the beam is in your own eye? Hypocrite, first take the beam out of your own eye, and then you will see clearly to take the speck out of your brother's eye."*

We have to remove the plank in our eye first before we can help someone else. Each depth of inner healing reveals things we had no idea of how that had been affecting us. A good friend of mine received the Word of the Lord concerning this. The Father spoke to her, saying, *"Heal the healers."* He went on to tell her that healing begins with us first. We have to be healed emotionally, physically, and spiritually before we can attempt to help another. The same goes for discernment. Discernment is a call to intercession, pure and simple. As we move into the revelation that comes from discernment, we are called to pray and intercede not only on behalf of others but for ourselves as well. This practice will keep us in humility.

If you need help with self discernment, ask for it. There is no shame or condemnation in asking for help. It doesn't mean you are weak. We are constantly bombarded with everything all at once in today's world that sneaky little foxes can slip in unawares. Even the most seasoned of us miss these foxes too. Seek the help of those you trust, and know are already operating in deep levels of discernment. Also, keep in mind that generational bloodline issues will always need to be dealt with. To help you in this, be mindful of these strategies:

- ➤ **Ask for prayer.** Always have a trusted friend or mentor interceding for you as you go through this process. It will help bring revelation and provide protection for you.
- ➤ **Seek the Lord.** Always seek the Lord first before proceeding into self discernment. Come to the place of total surrender to Him and His will for you.
- ➤ **Be still.** Sit quietly, listening to the voice of your Heavenly Father. Practicing stillness is one of the most amazing times of intimacy we can have as believers.
- ➤ **Give control to the work of the Holy Spirit.** Allow the Holy Spirit to invade every part of you, revealing what needs to be revealed. Allow some time for this as you listen. The key here is to listen and obey what He is telling you.
- ➤ **RRBB** *(Totally stole this phrase)*. Repent of what needs to be repented. Renounce what needs to be renounced. Break off what needs to be broken off. And, bless your spirit with the Word. Ask Yeshua for the verbiage you will need for this. Listen and be

obedient to say what you hear Him speak. What the Lord does in intimacy is one of the most potent times of inner healing you can have.

➢ **Confide in someone.** Confide in your friend about what happened during your time of self discernment. Doing this will help confirm you have dealt with what needed to be dealt with or if you need to revisit some areas. It may be necessary to have your friend on the phone with you as you go through this. I have trusted intercessors that I regularly call that work with me on this very thing.

Practical Application 1:

Try this simple activity to stretch your self discernment. Follow the prayer strategy outlined in this section. A dear prayer warrior friend of mine suggests grabbing a pen and notebook and lie in bed for this. You may choose whatever place you feel comfortable in. The bedroom does invite intimacy.

➢ Ask for prayer from trusted intercessors before you begin this exercise.

➢ Sit quietly for a few moments and then enter into worship.

➢ Begin to ask the Father about any areas of your life in which you need to deal.

➢ Be open to receiving direction and correction.

➢ Write down what the Father tells you and ask for strategies to break those things off.

➢ Write down how each of those things affects your body.

➢ Note the freedom you experience afterward.

➢ Worship the Father.

➢ Consult with a trusted mentor or friend what has been revealed and allow them to pray for you and with you.

➢ Let someone you trust discern you afterward. Doing this will help you identify something you may have missed.

➤ Repeat regularly.

Discerning Your Own Home

Discerning your own home may be a difficult task. Because we are so familiar with our house, we often miss spiritual squatters that have camped out there. There can be so many open doors to our homes that include visitors, electronic devices, what we watch on TV, the music we listen to, even our conversations and attitudes. Emotional stresses from our jobs, ministries, and day to day life can be an open door for the enemy. We must also consider the land our property connects to as well as our property could be a possible opening for the enemy. As a believer, you are more than able to discern your home and protect what the Lord has given you dominion over. Remember, you have full authority in your own home. You can apply the same guidelines above for your home. I strongly suggest having someone come to your home afterward to help you discern if everything has been dealt with. If you are uncomfortable discerning your home on your own, ask someone you trust to help you.

Discerning your home may be a bit more difficult and may require more intense prayer. Try this exercise to help you get started.

- ➢ Ask for a prayer covering from trusted intercessors before you begin this exercise.
- ➢ Leave your property and sit quietly at a local park. Seek the Lord while you are sitting in nature. You need to leave your home so you can properly align with the Father without the things to which you are accustomed to at home.
- ➢ Allow the refreshing of the Holy Spirit to come upon you and soak in it.
- ➢ Return home while listening to worship music on the way.
- ➢ Walk through your home and around the perimeter of your property with your senses attuned to the spirit realm.
- ➢ Write down what you are sensing.
- ➢ Ask the Lord for strategies to deal with what you are sensing.
- ➢ Follow the instructions of the Lord carefully.
- ➢ Once you are finished, release praise and worship in your home.
- ➢ Ask for a trusted friend or mentor to come and do a discernment walk-through of your home and property to see if you missed anything.
- ➢ Repeat regularly.

Discerning Others

There will be times that we are called to discern other people. Please do not go around discerning people at random and speaking to them about what you are sensing. This habit is an invasion of privacy. Discerning of others should only be done upon request. We need a clear understanding of what is and is not acceptable when discerning people. Discernment of others comes into play during deliverance and inner healing sessions. Once again, there is no room for presumptions and assumptions or preconceived judgments in discernment. This is especially true for those who are discerning other people and their homes or businesses. When it comes to discerning people, you must be very, very careful not to assume anything based on the intimate knowledge and experience you have concerning the person you are discerning. Allow all of it to go out the window and not allow that information to sway your discernment. Just because you may have known that a person has operated in witchcraft at one point in their life, does not mean you will sense that on them. The person could have already received deliverance in that area. Never assume.

I feel witchcraft in my head while discerning land and property, but that does not mean that I will feel witchcraft on someone else's head. If I am discerning someone and sense, in the spirit, something around or sitting on the person's head, that does not mean that they are operating in witchcraft. I take note of how what is on their head feels. I feel it using my non-dominate hand. I am looking for any sharp edges; if the item is smooth or not; if it is hard; does it feel like God or something dark. If I feel it on my head while discerning someone, then I can lean towards witchcraft coming against the person, or it is in their bloodline. It could be they are thinking through a witchcraft-type mindset.

If you discern something sitting on the person's head, do not assume this is witchcraft. Always, ask the Father what it is. Never assume anything. You could be feeling their helmet of salvation or a particular anointing this person is walking in. Listen to the voice of the Father concerning the person. Remember, we are to honor the person we are discerning not accuse them.

Here are some guidelines to keep in mind when discerning another person that will help you develop in this area:

> **Seek the Lord first and foremost before discerning someone.** If you are not in tune with the Father ahead of time, you could miss what He is telling you.

➤ **<u>Check yourself first.</u>** Close down your bloodline and ask the Father for sanctions against any open door in your life and bloodline, so it will not interfere with your discernment.

➤ **<u>You cannot allow yourself to be judgmental.</u>** Do not allow anything you already know or think you know about someone to cloud your discernment. Ask the Father to erase any preconceived notions you have concerning someone, so your discernment will be pure. You cannot correctly discern another with any angst in your heart or preconceived judgments in your mind against the person you are discerning. You have to take yourself out of the equation.

Practical Application 3:

Now that you have worked on self discernment, you are ready to advance to discerning others. It is best to discern someone with whom you have mutual trust. Do not assume anything just because you are familiar with your discernment buddy. This exercise is meant to be fun and engaging and not condemning or condescending in any way.

➤ Start by worshipping the Lord together.

➤ Choose who wants to go first and have that person sit in a chair in the center of the room or a place with enough space to walk around.

➤ Pray for your buddy.

➤ Begin discerning. Circle the chair while praying in the spirit and asking the Father to reveal what is hidden.

➤ Be honest with what you are sensing or not sensing.

➤ Ask the Father to let you feel the person's angels.

➤ Ask to sense the person's redemptive gift.

➤ Ask to sense your buddy's spirit and the anointing they carry.

➢ Ask the Father if any demonic entities are coming against this person and for revelation about those entities.

➢ Ask if there is any witchcraft coming against this person.

➢ Ask to sense any ungodly attachments (tags) in the spirit realm to your buddy.

➢ Write down how each feels.

➢ TO THE ONE BEING DISCERNED: Do not get offended by what the discerner tells you they are sensing. This information is for the benefit of both of you. Don't think, "I've already dealt with that" when you are told what the discerner is picking up.

➢ Pray and ask for strategies on how to deal with any witchcraft and entities. Keep in mind that it may not be anything you are called to remove from your buddy. It may become a point for inner healing for the individual later on.

➢ Switch places and let the other person go through the same process.

Discerning Other Places

For discerning other places, you need to make sure you have closed every door possible. Anything in the land can interfere with your discernment. Any unhealed place in you can also react to the land. Check with your team leader to see what renunciations will need to be done before going on a discernment mission. Yes, renunciations should be done even if you are going to discern. Here are a few strategies to help guide you:

➢ **Seek the Lord first.** Always seek the Lord when going into a home or business to discern. Make sure you are in tune with the heart of the Father. Obey if the Lord tells you not to go.

➢ **Check yourself first.** Shut every door and close off any generational iniquity in your bloodline that could interact with the land in which you are going. Make sure you are in unity with your team. Any angst against anyone in the group is an opening. Make sure you leave pressures of your job and home life at home.

➢ **<u>Do not make assumptions.</u>** Do not assume anything based on what you know or think you know about the place when you set your feet on the ground. You cannot jump to conclusions.

➢ **<u>Line it up.</u>** Someone on the team should have already done pre-prayer journey research. Does what you are sensing line up with the research? If not, it may be something that will need to be dug deeper into through more research. Do not assume your discernment is the final authority. You could be discerning something on one of the team members.

Practical Application 4:

Here is another fun exercise to do with a trusted friend and prayer partner. For this application exercise, you will be stretching your discernment differently. You will be discerning where to discern as well as a variety of different things to discern once you are boots on the ground. Remember this is just a discernment mission ONLY. This mission is not a prayer assignment. Think of it as going behind enemy lines to gather intel. Remember to turn off all distractions.

➢ Gather with your partner and enter into worship.

➢ Pray and cover yourselves in the Blood of Yeshua asking for any open doors to be closed and your bloodline to be silent as you discern.

➢ Seek the Lord as to where to discern. You can do this apart from each other, making it all the more fun. If you choose to do this, write down on a piece of paper where you feel the Lord is leading you, place it in an envelope, and seal it. Keep the location secret from each other. Lay your envelopes on the table and discern which envelope to open.

➢ Once your location has been revealed, pray en route and worship.

➢ Stay together with your friend at all times.

➢ Ask the Lord to discern the angels at the location.

➢ Ask to be able to feel a Godly gate.

➢ Ask to be able to feel a Godly gatekeeper.

➢ Note how your body reacts to each.

➢ Ask the Father to allow you to feel an ungodly door/portal in the spirit realm.

➢ Ask to be able to feel an ungodly gate.

➢ Ask to be able to feel an ungodly gatekeeper.

➢ Note how your body reacts to each.

> ➢ Ask Jesus to remove all ungodly things from your presence.

> ➢ Praise and thank the Father for allowing you to experience these things.

> ➢ Do not be upset if you feel absolutely nothing the first time you try this or even the next few times. It is a process.

> ➢ As you leave, worship.

Practical Application 5:

For this exercise, you will need at least four friends and a couple of days to experience this one fully. Take your time, and do not be afraid to make mistakes. Remember, you are learning.

> ➢ Decide on a place to discern.

> ➢ Break off into groups of two and decide on a day that each group will discern the chosen location.

> ◆ One group will discern the Godly angelic, portals, gates and ley lines, etc.

> ◆ The second group will discern the demons, ungodly portals, gates and ley lines, etc.

> ◆ Take as accurate notes as possible as to the locations of each thing you are discerning.

> ➢ Come back together and compare notes.

Discerning With a Group

There will be times that you may be called to discern with a group as part of a broader assignment. Always, always, always stay in formation and be obedient to the authority of the team leader. When you extend honor to those who have authority over you, it brings the Glory as well as a deeper level of protection for you and the team. *(The practical application for this will be done in the field under the guidance of your team leader.)* These strategies will help you grow and develop in this area:

> **Always, always, always follow the lead of your team leader.** Coming out from under the authority of your leadership will open you up for backlash and attack. You have to abide by what the leaders are telling you. Respect and honor your spiritual covering. Honor brings the Glory.

> **Stay on mission.** Going off mission and attempting to tackle something you have not researched on is highly dangerous for yourself as well as the rest of the team. Stay in formation. Just because the Father reveals something or an entity shows itself, does not mean that is your assignment for that particular time. If you are only there to discern, then discern **ONLY** no matter what manifests.

> **Stay together as a team.** If you are assigned a discernment buddy, stay with that person for the entire time you are discerning. Do not wander off. This practice is for your safety.

> **Do not takeover.** Do not take over leading the team. You are part of the team and not in control. The team does not answer to you, you answer to your team leader.

> **Do not feel like you have to find everything.** You will wear yourself out. We all miss things. Do not beat yourself up or be upset because you didn't sense something. You are part of a team, and as a team, you will all pick up on different elements in the spirit realm.

➢ **Pay attention to how the team members are discerning.** Learn from each other and cue off each other's discernment. What does that mean, cue off each other's discernment? If you know that a particular team member reacts a certain way around the demonic, move closer to them to see if you can sense what it is and hone in on it.

➢ **Do not compare yourself to anyone else who is in the group.** Comparison is not only a confidence killer but a faith-killer. God has gifted you, never doubt it. God uniquely made you, and you operate differently than everyone else. You have a place and are accepted. And, so is your gifting.

➢ **Respect your fellow team members.** Do not distract them by idle chit-chat nor poke or touch your fellow team members. Do not yell across the room or raise your voice to gain the attention of the team unless you are under attack.

➢ **It is okay to question, just do not disrupt.** Pretend you are in school and raise your hand if you have a question. Please DO NOT blurt questions out during a discernment mission. It is a distraction. You may quietly ask the lead if they can help discern what you are feeling. Everything must be done appropriately. If you do not want to ask your question out loud, make a note of it, and seek the Lord about it after the assignment is over. If necessary, ask for prayer from the group afterwards, so you can receive the revelation as to what you were sensing.

➢ **Do not hold back.** If you are sensing something, you need to give it a voice. Do not be afraid to share what you are sensing, even if it seems strange or goes against what someone else is sensing. For those who are new to operating in discernment as a group, do not be afraid to say what you are discerning even if it doesn't make sense in the natural.

➢ **Do not argue.** Do not argue about what you are sensing with another member of the team. Discord and division create an open door for the enemy. You can disagree

44

without conflict, strive for unity at all times.

➢ **<u>Never forget to take notes.</u>** Taking notes will help you as you grow in your discernment. It will also help you if you go back to this location on a prayer assignment.

Chapter Six
Blockages to Discernment

Some times our discernment is blocked, and we cannot function. We chalk our not being able to operate in our God-given discernment as *"I am just not gifted in that area."* The truth is, we are all gifted in discernment. We do not walk in the fullness of what God has given us. In this chapter, we will explore some of the things the enemy uses to block our discernment and ways to overcome them. This list is by no means an exhaustive one. Many, many things can cause us not to be able to operate in our discernment. If you are experiencing difficulty in the areas of discernment, this chapter will hopefully highlight the possible culprits of you not being able to function in your God-given ability of discernment.

Lack of Intimacy

Lack of intimacy with our Father can create a variety of issues in our lives. Our spiritual livelihood and strength depend on our intimacy with our Heavenly Father. If we lack in any area of our spiritual intimacy with Him, our lives unravel thread by thread. It is only through intimacy with God the Father we become able to distinguish between Him and the enemy.

Keeping our Word life healthy, offering praise and worship, communing with Him in prayer, and fellowshipping with other believers will keep us sharpened and honed in. Never underestimate the power of being in communion with one another. Proverbs 27:17 says, *"As iron sharpens iron, so a person sharpens the countenance of his friend."* It is only in the confines of covenantal relationships that the sharpening happens. Within covenantal relationships, there is deep trust in each other. With trust comes safety. Our relationships with fellow believers are a safe place for us to be real and experience God together.

We cannot discern by the spirit and by the Word if we are not in on-going intimacy with the Father. God is Spirit (John 4:24), and Yeshua is the Living Word (John 1:14). We cannot partner with the Yeshua if we do not know Him. He is the source of our gifts and callings. Look at it this way; you have this exquisitely beautiful Tiffany lamp that you never plugged in the outlet. Lamps are designed to bring light; however, it will never bring light unless you connect it to the flow of electricity. That is how it is with us. We were designed to bring the Light to the world, but we will never shine His light if we are not in His presence regularly. Living from Sunday to Wednesday and Wednesday to Sunday without any fellowship in between makes for a very weak and dim Christian. We cannot correctly discern our Heavenly Father from the enemy if we are not continually in the presence of our Heavenly Father through communing with Him in prayer and worship and by being in the Word. Apart from Him, we can do nothing (John 15:5).

Not Knowing Your Spiritual Identity

A lack of intimacy with the Father will cause us to lose sight of our identity. We will never walk in our authority if we do not know our identity. Thomas Fazekas writes, "*Without knowing our personal identity we are much like a rudderless ship drifting aimlessly on the ocean, subject to the whims of the tides and winds.*"[1]

We will never operate in our gifting if we have any misconception of our identity. But what is *"identity?"* The Merriam-Webster dictionary defines *"identity"* as:

> "*the distinguishing character or personality of an individual : individuality; the relation established by psychological identification; the condition of being the same with something described or asserted establish the identity of stolen goods; sameness of essential or generic character in different instances; sameness in all that constitutes the objective reality of a thing : oneness.*"

Our identity is what makes us who we are. It is comprised of our characteristics, strengths, weaknesses, and gifts. Our identity is who we are. It is a constant in our lives that will unfold before us like a flower in Spring as we develop and grow. It is not what we do. Our early life experiences and circumstances can shape ourselves. Say, for instance, you had an abusive childhood, your self-worth and identity will be tied to being accepted by others. When we are unable to be in direct fellowship with God, we take our identity in who others say we are, our circumstances, our jobs, etc.

As a woman, it is so easy to be caught up in believing our identity is in our marriage, children, home life, or career. Men can easily attempt to find their identity in their jobs, the money they make, the cars they drive, the type of women they attract, etc. These are not our identity. These things are what we do, not who we are. We were created first for intimacy with the Father. It is from that divine communion with Him that we truly discover who we are.

We have a physical identity as well as a spiritual identity. Our physical identity comes from our genetic makeup – our inherited characteristics from our father and mother. Our spiritual identity, however, comes only from our Heavenly Father. And this is where the enemy will fight against us the most. He knows we will become highly dangerous if we discover and begin to walk in our true spiritual identity. When we start to understand our identity, we learn of what weapons and benefits we have at our disposal through Christ.

Our spiritual identity supersedes our physical identity. We must live out our spiritual identity in a physical realm. How do we do that exactly? Yeshua is the perfect example of doing just that. He lived out His spiritual identity in the physical realm. Yeshua was fully man – the Son of Mary and Joseph, and yet fully God – the Word made flesh, Son of God, the Messiah. He lived out His spiritual identity by fulfilling His calling here on the Earth. When we live boldly in reckless abandon, total obedience to the Father and do His will, we are manifesting our identity as a son of the Most High God. Jesus said He did nothing that He did not see the Father do (John 5:19). There was intimacy between the Father and the Son that allowed Yeshua to live out of His spiritual identity. Take some time to study out who the Bible says you are. Repent for not accepting and receiving your spiritual identity. Then ask the Father for grace to receive your spiritual identity and to walk it out. As you grow in intimacy with the Father, your sense of identity becomes rooted and grounded in His love and Word. Living in your true identity will empower you to operate in your gifts and callings.

Wrong Perception of Self-Worth and God's Love

We can read scripture on how much the Father loves us and have a good working head knowledge of it, but not necessarily grasp the depth of that love in our spirits. Our issue lies in our acceptance of the belief that the Father loves us unconditionally. Our tainted view of our self-worth and His love for us causes us to doubt our discernment abilities.

The conceptual principle of God's love is made evident in scripture repeatedly. We believe all scripture to be true and the very breath of God. Our acceptance of those truths is more the utilization of those truths and not necessarily shaped by any evidence or evidential reasoning on the scripture.

Just because I believe the evidence presented in scripture to be true that God is love and that I am infinitely loved has no bearing on the acceptance of the fact God loves me infinitely. Religion has taught us that we should work to gain God's love and favor.

Children have no issue accepting the fact that their parents love them until evidence reveals otherwise causing a shift in their acceptance of the beliefs now proven wrong. So, the root issue is shown to be a war of the heart knowledge (acceptance) and head knowledge (belief).

The outlying factors, or weapons of war the enemy uses to cause the conflict of belief and acceptance, are tactical in nature, consisting of perception – how we view ourselves and the world around us. Perception is 90% of reality. Our perception of self-worth creates our reality of God's love for us. If the enemy can shift our focus to us being unworthy of what God has freely given us, then the fight for our core beliefs has all but been won.

To move from a defeated acceptance of *"the Bible is true, but I am not good enough for scriptures to be true for me"* to the full acceptance of *"the Bible is true, and I am worthy of the promises held within scripture"* is no easy feat. Breaking the barrier of heart knowledge and head knowledge is a work best left to the Holy Spirit for it cannot be done in our human strength or force of will.

Submission is not an inherent human trait, but an act of will. As a child submits to parental authority, so we too must give way to God's authority relinquishing our rights and let Him shatter the barriers so that scriptural truths become our reality. Sound too easy? It really is that simple.

I will not lie to you. I ask daily for the Father to help me accept His truth concerning His love. Yes, daily. There are days I question my acceptance of those truths. And, daily, I put to death those false beliefs.

I want to address the women who are reading this. There is a great lie force-fed to us as women by religious dogma. We are taught that our gender prevents us from being anything more than a wife and mother. We are told we cannot preach from the pulpit or be graced with the five-fold ministry gifts because we are women. Our self-worth is captured by this lie and warps the view of the Father's love for us. Even though scripture clearly states that there is neither male nor female (Galatians 3:28), the concept of female being less than male has been ingrained in us. The idea of God loving us enough to save us, but not to bless us with the Gifts of the Spirit is painted into a hideous false portrait of our self-worth. This is the animosity with which Satan rages against women. If he can cause women to look down upon herself, then she will never produce.

I have walked this road. I found myself begging God to love me because I had been told the

50

lie that I was not good enough to be used and loved of God because I was a woman. All of those negative thoughts and gender-based self-hatred culminated and manifested into a spirit of depression and suicide that raged against me for years. I struggled in abusive relationship after abusive relationship looking for some resemblance of what love looked like, especially a father's love. Even after salvation, this on-going battle raged. I had no love identity. Through it all, Father God was still doting on me. He was trying to break through as I could see myself as He saw me.

There have been times His love gave me a denial of something I wanted that I had to reconcile. I saw His denial or delay as a lack of love, but it was out of His love for me He denied and delayed. It was through those times that He loved me the most. I am seeing, even now, when there is a delay or what I perceive as a *"no"* from Papa, it is His protective love for me in action. There is protection in His love and mercy.

Performance-based love breeds fear. 1 John 4:18 gives us an accurate picture of God's love. The scripture states, *"There is no fear in love, but perfect love drives out fear. For fear has to do with punishment, and the one who fears has not been made perfect in love."*

The Greek word used for the first "perfect" in this scripture is the word *"teleios,"* which means "complete and wanting nothing, finished." The second *"perfect"* is the Greek word *"teleioo,"* which means "to make complete, accomplish, to complete, fulfillment, to bring to the end proposed." God's love for us makes us perfect for His use and perfect to receive that love. We are made for Him to love us and that love to flow through us.

We, as women, have a great call in the Body of Christ to produce the seeds of revival. Women are natural birthers. What we birth in prayer for Him cannot be hushed nor silenced. Look at Lucy Farrow, who provided the initial spark that ignited the Azuza Street revival. It is written of her that no one spoke in tongues until she arrived and began laying hands on and praying for the people that the baptism of the Holy Spirit began to be poured out. Her role was so pivotal that the January 1908 issue of Apostolic Faith magazine wrote about the role of women during this great outpouring:

> *"Before Pentecost, the woman could only go into the 'court of the women' and not into the inner court. But when our Lord poured out Pentecost, He brought all those faithful women with the other disciples into the upper room, and God baptized them all in the same room and made no difference. All the women received the anointed oil of the Holy Ghost and were able to preach the same as men. They both were co-workers in Eden, and both fell into sin; so they both have to come together and work in the Gospel."[2]*

We have to come to the realization that He loves us and wants to love us. We have to be willing to receive and accept that love. Let His love flood you, and allow Him to tell you how proud He is of you. And yet, there is still a deeper *"yes"* that He will lead us to.

If you are in the place of recognizing yourself as having an incorrect view of your self-worth and His love for you, then, by all means, seek inner healing immediately. We must be set free to be able to discern through the correct lens.

Fear

Fear is the most efficient blockage the enemy has against our discernment. It is the sneakiest and the most deadly. I have heard FEAR stands for *"False Evidence Appearing Real." "Forget Everything And Run."* I have also heard that *"fear is the opposite of faith."* In actuality, fear is the absence of love. 1 John 4:8 tells us that *"perfect love drives out fear"* further revealing that fear is the opposite of love. Fear comes from a lack of intimacy with the Father and a lack of knowing our identity in Christ.

It is very easy to get into fear with our discernment, especially as you are growing. As our new spiritual receiver goes up, we pick up on every single thing. For the majority of people, this is can be very frightening. And, understandably so. Fear will cause us to plead with the Lord to shut off our discernment. It is Fear that will cause us to step back from our gifting. Do not do that. We are issued a strong warning about pulling back out of fear in Hebrews 10:38 (AMP), *"But the just shall live by faith [My righteous servant shall live by his conviction respecting man's relationship to God and divine things, and holy fervor born of faith and conjoined with it]; and if he draws back and shrinks in fear, My soul has no delight or pleasure in him."*

Fear is such a paralyzing agent and is one of the most powerful tools of the enemy. If we are not sufficiently rooted and grounded in the perfect love of God, fear can slip in. Generational fear robs us from fulfilling our destinies in Christ. God's desire for us is to come to a full revelation of His love for us so we can live out *"perfect love drives out fear"* (1 John 4:18).

If you are finding yourself overcome with fear as you discern, this could be an indicator of a generational issue. Contact a qualified inner healing and deliverance minister immediately.

Unfulfilled Expectations

Unfulfilled expectations on ourselves and others can hinder our discernment. When we do not get our way about something, our feelings are hurt. We are offended and hurt when people do not perform for us the way we expect them to. When God does not answer in the manner or timetable we expect, we get mad and feel rejected. Our gaze darkens; our heads droop downward; we walk a bit slower. Rejection creeps in and decides to camp out. The longer we entertain rejection, the more our discernment is tainted by it. Placing unrealistic expectations on ourselves, others and God will always bring frustration.

Our expectations are predominately founded on our emotional state, wrong teachings, our woundings, and selfish desires. Expectations founded on these faulty principles will always be unmet, leaving us frustrated. Expectations founded on scripture are always met. Based on scripture, we can always expect the Father to be present, good, loving, accepting of us even when we make a mistake, and forgiving. We understand that God's timing is not ours. His wisdom is above ours. He does not go around granting wishes, but answering faith. We tend to misuse Psalm 37:5, which states, *"Delight yourself in Adonai, and He will give you the requests of your heart."* We forget the next verse. Psalm 37:5 states, *"Commit your way to Adonai. Trust in Him, and He will do it."* We have to commit to His way and take pleasure in Him first.

Looking at the Hebrew words in these two verses will significantly help you to understand how our expectations should be set concerning the Father. The word for *"delight"* is *"anag,"* which means *"to be delicate, soft, be pampered by, take exquisite delight, to be merry over."* The word for *"give"* is the Hebrew word *"nathan,"* which means *"to be entrusted with as to give an account of."* Whoa! God only gives us what we are able to steward. Stop expecting God to provide you with a Bentley when you are only able to steward a Pinto!

The word used for *"heart"* is *"leb,"* which means *"inner man, soul, the seat of appetites and emotions."* The word "commit" is *"galal,"* which means to *"roll over or away, to flow."* To be able to receive the desires of our heart, we must be willing to roll away our plans and agendas for God's. There has to be an exchange first.

Expectations of people are a different animal. We expect people to behave and react based on our set of standards. When they do not, we are disappointed in them. As parents, we expect specific behavior from our children. When they misbehave, we are disappointed but still extend grace to them. This extension of grace should be the norm for everyone whom we have placed realistic and healthy expectations. Even if we base our expectations on scripture, whereas people are concerned, people will always disappoint us. Scripture tells us the flesh is corrupt. The flesh will always reap flesh. Just because someone is a Christian does not mean their lives fully line up with scripture. If a Christian has proven themselves to be untrustworthy, you can expect that person to be untrustworthy until they prove themselves otherwise.

Placing unrealistic expectations on people who are not at the level of our expectations for them is highly frustrating. That is where grace should abound. We should be bearing with one another and forgiving of them when they do not meet our expectations (Colossians 3:12).

If we are truly being changed from Glory to Glory, we can expect the good things of God to come forth out of us with a bit of *"flavor"* from the pipe along with it. As we are being transformed into the image of His son, there will always be things in us that surface and give place to disappointment not only to ourselves but to others.

Base our expectations for ourselves, others, and God off scripture first. We must first meet those expectations ourselves before we can enforce them on others. If we expect someone to respect us, we should be respectable and seek to give respect. If we want someone to be loving towards us, we must first be loving towards others. We expect people to show us grace when we mess up but are we extending that same grace to others when they mess up?

The realization of the only expectations on us from the Father is to *"only believe"* frees us from the disappointment caused by religion that teaches us to by all means *"be perfect."* It is not a work for us to accomplish. God Himself perfects us. We cannot be perfect or achieve perfection through religious ritual or rigorous and dogmatic views of the perception of holiness.

Personal Iniquity

Sin will always keep us from the fullness of what God has for us (Isaiah 59:2). When we are in sin, our gifts will not correctly operate. It is not that our gifts have been taken away, but sin has placed a barrier in our way.

Romans 6:12-13 says, *"Therefore do not let sin rule in your mortal body so that you obey its desires. And do not keep yielding your body parts to sin as tools of wickedness; but yield yourselves to God as those alive from the dead, and your body parts as tools of righteousness to God."*

If we are in sin, we are not operating in the life that the Father has for us, and our discernment will be clogged. Our sin can do one of two things - shut down our discernment or distort it. The majority of the time, it will be shut down. There is the rare occasion that our discernment becomes distorted. When our discernment becomes distorted, it usually is because we are operating in a critical and judgmental spirit.

Repentance brings refreshing, and our gift will begin to bloom again. Acts 3:19-20 (AMP) states:

> *"So repent [change your inner self—your old way of thinking, regret past sins]*
> *and return [to God—seek His purpose for your life], so that your sins may be*
> *wiped away [blotted out, completely erased], so that times of refreshing may*
> *come from the presence of the Lord [restoring you like a cool wind on a hot day];*
> *and that He may send [to you] Jesus, the Christ, who has been appointed for*
> *you."*

Repent of what needs to be repented. Renounce what needs to be renounced. Break off what needs to be broken off. Then, release scriptural blessings over yourself. Sound too simple? Well, it is just that simple. If you need deeper cleansing, seek out a deliverance minister for inner healing.

Bloodlines, Generational Iniquities and Our DNA

We cannot stress enough the power our bloodlines have over us. Members of our ancestry who have entered into agreements with the demonic cause curses to come upon us. Each of these agreements is legally binding in the Courts of Heaven and must be dealt with in the Courts. A strong occultic bloodline will cause the generations to be pulled into the occult. Unfortunately, not enough people give credence to this. Exodus 20:5 says, *"Do not bow down to them, do not let anyone make you serve them. For I, Adonai your God, am a jealous God, bringing the iniquity of the fathers upon the children to the third and fourth generations of those who hate Me,"*

Isaiah 65:6-7 repeats this same warning,

> *"Behold, it is written before Me; I will not keep silence but will repay, even repay into their laps, your iniquities, and the iniquities of your fathers together,' says Adonai, 'because they burned incense on the mountains, and scorned Me on the hills. So I will measure into their laps full wages for their former deeds'."*

This warning is also echoed in Jeremiah 31:29, Ezekiel 18:2, and Job 21:19. It is a reoccurring theme. We must deal with our bloodlines or else it will deal with us. The occult knows this principle as well. Practitioners will scan people's bloodlines looking for ways to manipulate them. How do they *"scan?"* Through discernment. Yes, the occult operates in a very high-level form of discernment. They are always looking for a way to manipulate people through their bloodlines. If a Christian is operating as a true son of God and is in the way of occult practitioners, they will start looking at the bloodlines of that person for openings in the generations that can be used as an open door for an attack to bring an end to the threat.

The occult is always on the lookout for power bloodlines. Power bloodlines are those of the descendants of royalty, high-level occultists, and powerful political families. Say, for instance, you are from a power bloodline like a long line of shamans. The occult can pick up on that bloodline and seek a way to use it for their benefit. This can be done in a variety of ways. The occult can entrap a person born of a power bloodline by use of sex magic, associations, and occult involvement.

Through sex magic, an occult practitioner will create a marriage covenant in the spirit realm with a person of a powerful bloodline. It creates a spirit husband or spirit wife. Because in the spirit realm two become one, the practitioner now has a full legal right to tap into everything that person has in their bloodline. Occultists can even connect to other people utilizing the one they have ensnared with sex magic. Each subsequent person, the first person, connects with sexually links back to the practitioner, giving the practitioner more power. So, in essence, the practitioner has his or her private harem of spiritual batteries to tap. Remember everything you are still connected to in the spirit realm in this way links to your spouse in the marriage bed.

To remove generational and bloodline iniquities will take time, patience, and deliverance. You will need experienced people to help you through deliverance and inner healing. You will require someone skilled in navigating in the Courts of Heaven to receive divorce decrees from anyone connected to you as a spirit husband or spirit wife.

The occult understands the power of blood. Life is in the blood. Everything that we are is in our DNA. Our DNA contains the memories of our ancestors. All of this is useful to the occult. Occultists will use the DNA of people for all sorts of nefarious reasons and will go to extremes to get their hands on anything containing your DNA such as blood samples, strands of hair, and fingernail clippings. Spells are more powerful when bound by blood and carry greater weight in the spirit realm. They can manipulate people, cause illnesses, bring financial ruin, etc. just by using DNA.

In the case of your DNA being used against you, you can pray and have your DNA burned up and rendered unusable in the fire of the Holy Spirit. At salvation, we receive a spiritual blood transfusion. We then carry the DNA of God Himself. Declare that over yourself. Command your DNA to come into agreement and be purified by the powerful Blood of Yeshua.

Contaminated Land

There are times when the land itself will prevent you from operating in discernment. Why? There is something in the land connecting with something in your bloodline preventing you

58

from operating in your gifting. Iniquities in the land will definitely agree with unhealed places in our bloodlines and our sins. This reason is why you never discern land alone. How do we combat this? Make an effort to seek inner healing continually. We will be going through inner healing from now until the Lord returns. It is not something to be dreaded but enjoyed. It may be painful as you begin, but the rewards of living in freedom far outweigh any personal discomfort.

If you are wondering how the land can be contaminated, the Bible is very clear on what defiles the land. Bloodshed, idolatry, sins of the people, breaking covenants, occult practices, worship of other gods, and sexual sins pollute the land. These sins will cause the generational sins in our bloodlines to clash or agree with one another. These clashes and agreements cause our bodies to react in negative ways.

Ungodly Soul Ties

A soul tie is an attachment of our soul to another person, a place or thing. These connections involve both our thoughts and emotions and the choices we make. The most dangerous of these is between two people. God designed us to have connection one to another. We are spirit as well as physical. Our spirits were designed to be godly and healthily connected with other people's spirit.

People argue that soul ties are not biblical. The Bible does not use the term *"soul tie,"* but it does illustrate the concept. Genesis 34:1-3 highlights the concept of soul ties:

> *"Now Dinah, Leah's daughter, whom she bore for Jacob, went out to look at the daughters of the land. When Shechem the son of Hamor the Hivite, the prince of the land, saw her, he took her and lay with her and raped her. But his soul clung to Dinah, Jacob's daughter, and he loved the young woman and spoke reassuringly to the young woman."*

This scripture gives us an example of an ungodly soul tie created through sexual intercourse. The word for *"clung"* is the Hebrew word *"dabaq"* which means *"to cling, or adhere; to catch by pursuit: abide fast, cleave (fasten together), follow close (hard after), be joined (together), overtake, pursue hard, stick, take."* Shechem's soul, in essence, abided with Dinah.

Ungodly soul ties influence our emotions in negative ways. Be careful of who you allow into your inner circle. The spirit in operation in a person can begin to influence us. Therefore the warning in Psalm 1:1 would not have been included in the Bible. It states, *"Happy is the one who has not walked in the advice of the wicked, nor stood in the way of sinners, nor sat in the seat of scoffers."*

I was raised on the old saying, *"If you lie down with dogs, you'll wake up with fleas."* This statement is echoed in 1 Corinthians 15:33, which states, *"Do not be deceived! 'Bad company corrupts good morals.'"* The Common English Translation of this verse says, *"Don't fool yourselves. Bad friends will destroy you."*

Sometimes we place ourselves into relationships to help bring another person up. Instead, they bring us down. It is far easier for someone to pull us down than it is for us to bring that one up, especially if the other party is more interested in their selfish desires. Soul ties are very subtle. If we become attentive to the voice of these people, we begin to think as they do. We act as they do. We become like them. Be mindful of ungodly soul ties.

But what does it look like to have a Godly soul tie? 1 Samuel 18:1 says, *"Now it came to pass, when David had finished speaking to Saul, Jonathan's soul was knit to David's soul, and Jonathan loved him as himself."* This scripture is the very first mention of a non-sexual connection woven in the spirit between two people in a Godly manner. The word *"knit"* is the Hebrew word *"qashar,"* which means *"to tie, to physically confine or compact together in a league of love; to knit stronger together."* This word is only used in this instance in the Bible.

We were made for a covenantal experience with God and with each other. Jonathan and

David were in covenant with each other and looked after each other. That is a picture of what God intended for us. I highly recommend David Huskins' book *The Power of a Covenant Heart* for a deeper understanding of the subject of covenant.

If you find yourself realizing you have ungodly soul ties, seek deliverance. Allow the work of the Holy Spirit to be active in your life. Inner healing and deliverance will always bring these things to light and help in breaking you free from ungodly soul ties.

Spiritual Bullying and the Religious Spirit

The Western church, as a whole, does a great disservice both to individuals who are highly sensitive to the spirit realm and who have come out of the darkness of occult practice. It is called spiritual abuse and a religious spirit. Spiritual or religious abuse is *"a kind of abuse which damages the central core of who we are. It leaves us spiritually discouraged and emotionally cut off from the healing love of God."*[1] It can also be defined as *"the mistreatment of a person who is in need of help, support or greater spiritual empowerment, with the result of weakening, undermining, or decreasing that person's spiritual empowerment."*[2]

Spiritual abuse, or what I term *"spiritual bullying,"* can crush new and seasoned Christians alike. It opens the person up to a spirit of rejection. It causes them to stop in their tracks, and the hurt becomes an offense. If left un-dealt with, the offense can become bitterness. Once bitterness sets in, their love walk dries up and dies.

The religious spirit seeks to box people in and control them. It causes us to have a set standard for others to measure up to while extending grace only to ourselves. If others do not act like us, do not speak what we are speaking, think as we think, then we chastise them claiming they are not of us. The religious spirit shuts down the prophetic and the supernatural. The *"that doesn't happen today,"* saying gets tossed around at people who are zealous for the Lord.

I once overheard two older women talking about a very vibrant young woman who had just gotten saved. In their conversation, they were downing this woman's zeal and fire for the Lord. One of the ladies said to the other one, *"Give her a few years, and she will calm down. If she doesn't, the pastor will set her straight."* Seriously? *"Give her a few years, and she will calm down."* Let that sink in for a moment. What a word curse to release over this young woman, who by the way, ended up backsliding because people started telling her she needed to calm down and be quiet. They handed her a list of how she had to behave in church. Why? Because she was a threat. She was a threat because her fire was revealing their cold ash! She fell due to spiritual bullies. Not everyone who backslides does so because they want to. They go back to what they came from because they find death in the church due to religious, man-made rules. Religion kills relationship!

Religion will destroy an organization faster than most anything else. This spirit opens the doors for pride, rebellion, and Jezebel. It seeks to control and contain the gifts of the spirit under the pretense that only a few can obtain the gifts and callings of the Lord.

A religious spirit seeks its way instead of God's way. When a person operating in a religious spirit sees another being promoted due to their gifts, he or she will seek to destroy the reputation of the other and will go after the leader who is promoting the other person. Their thinking is that the one being promoted is somehow unworthy of that promotion. Someone controlled by a religious spirit is caught up in promotion and titles. They are blind to their spiritual bankruptcy. They throw out baseless accusations towards anyone they can to make themselves look good. Gossip and slander are commonplace within religious structures and may even be allowed with the false belief that knowing more dirt on a person will result in being able to pray for them more effectively. A critical spirit slips in under the guise of being *"prophetic"* or *"discerning."* Spiritual bullies will always go after those with whom they feel threatened.

Within the atmosphere of a religious spirit, those who are seeking healing are immediately disqualified from service by spiritual bullies. Those bullies say, *"If you aren't doing it this way or that way like I did, you are not doing it right." "If you aren't following this 5-step program put out by pastor such-and-such, then you are not clean enough to be used." "If our leader is promoting that person, then we need to confront him/her because they are being deceived."* Any of that sound familiar? If so, quickly repent! Make it right, now! And I mean NOW! A house divided cannot stand (Mark 3:25).

I have been a victim of spiritual bullying for the majority of my saved life. I have had people treat me like what I have done for the Lord is nothing compared to what they have done. There will always be those who are caught up in a religious spirit that will think no one can pray as well as they can or be used of the Lord the way they are. No one can have dreams that have as deep of spiritual meaning as they can. They pray for the sick and the sick recover, so God is so much more pleased with them than you leading someone to Christ. Your job is to maintain a pure heart in all you do, even in the face of ridicule and accusations.

Once people find out what God has delivered me from, they try and use it as a weapon to discredit me from being used in the Body of Christ. For years, my involvement in the occult was a source of deep shame for me. Church people would make fun of me and ridicule me about it. They would look at me with deep suspicion and prejudice.

You see, I walked in a very dark place for a good many years. Even though I was brought up in a God-fearing, Christian home, I struggled with my own spiritual walk. I knew God through religious ritual, rules, and regulations, but I didn't have a heart knowledge of who He was. He was not yet real to me. It wasn't until a horrifying experience, with a spell gone wrong against someone, that I realized where I really was. I began my search for the truth. Then on March 28, 1999, I surrendered to a God I had never known. Out of my lack of wisdom, I would tell people from what God had delivered me. That is when fellow Christians began to inflict a type of spiritual bullying upon me. It was as if somehow, being involved in the occult was an unforgivable sin to them.

What I learned in my past are now weapons in my arsenal against the enemy. I know how he operates, his tactics, and strategies. And I fully intend on using those things against him every chance I get. I am no longer ashamed of where I came from and what I did. I am standing on this side of the Cross in full recognition of what God has brought me from and the power it took to get me there. My next set of statements will come across as prideful to a person with a religious spirit, but these things must be said. I, now, fully understand Paul's statement to the Corinthian church when he said,*"I think it a small thing to be judged by you"* (1 Corinthians 4:3). I am secure in Him and my identity that the approval of those around me has no bearing on who I am and how I move in the spirit. I am secure enough in my anointing and calling that I need anyone to critique me based on their set of standards.

If you have been a victim of spiritual bullying, it is by no means a reflection of who you are, but rather a revealing marker as to their spiritual condition. You are only responsible for how you handle their accusations. You are not responsible for correcting your accusers. The Bible tells us to pray for those who are abusing you (Matthew 5:44). Release forgiveness to those who are being spiritual bullies. Pray Psalms over them and blessings. Do good to them and do not take revenge upon them (Romans 12:19-20). Always walk in love, no matter how hard it is.

Pride and Jealousy

Pride and jealousy are twin discernment killers. They tend to walk side-by-side and hand-in-hand. This dynamic duo of the enemy can shut you down in every area of your gifting, not just discernment. They will bring you down and destroy you. We need to look no further than the story of Cain and Abel in the fourth chapter of Genesis to see this laid out before us.

The *"Green-Eyed Monster"* of jealousy rears its ugly head in all ministries just like it does in business and politics. When we begin to compare ourselves to others and their gifting, we open the door wide for jealousy to enter. It will absolutely destroy you.

James 3:14-16 gives us this somber warning, *"But if you have bitter jealousy and selfish ambition in your heart, do not boast and lie against the truth. This is not the wisdom that comes down from above but is earthly, unspiritual, demonic. For where jealousy and selfish ambition exist, there is disorder and every evil practice."*

This verse calls jealousy what it is – demonic. A murderous spirit comes with the spirit of jealousy. We usually do not go around killing those who we are jealous of, but we do murder them with our words. Just as with pride, jealousy leads us to the path of character assassinations. We become critical and judgmental. We find fault in everything others do. We pick them apart behind their backs and then cause others to see the objects of our ridicule in a negative light.

Even being prideful in our discernment will cause us to stop functioning in our discernment. Being jealous of another person's discernment will cause ours to stop. We must always remind ourselves not to compare our gifting with another's. Comparison kills the anointing.

Being prideful in our strength and power will be our downfall. It was pride that brought down Lucifer after all. Pride caused so many of the people we read about in the Bible to fail. Pride is sneaky. It goes utterly undetected by us but evident to those around us. We usually do not recognize our pridefulness until we fall. Proverbs 16:18 says, *"Pride goes before destruction and a haughty spirit before a fall."* Pride will always cause you to fall no matter who you are or at what level you are.

Pride and jealousy make us character assassins. Often, people walking in pride and jealousy themselves accuse others of being prideful and jealous. This blame game keeps prying eyes off them and focuses the attention onto others. It calls into question the character and motives of others. It invites a critical spirit, the Absalom spirit, and Leviathan. All of which opens the door for Jezebel.

Be mindful of your accusations against others. Keep a watch over your words. Ephesians 4:29 says, *"Let no harmful word come out of your mouth, but only what is beneficial for building others up according to the need so that it gives grace to those who hear it."*

Philippians 2:3 reminds us, *"Do nothing out of selfishness or conceit, but with humility consider others as more important than yourselves."* Remember, love does not misbehave nor seeks out its own way, keeps no records of wrongs and rejoices in the truth (1 Corinthians 13:5-6). If we are truly walking in love one with another, we will not falsely accuse another. Ask a trusted friend to keep you accountable and humble. Repent quickly of any pridefulness and murderous words you have spoken even if you cannot see where you have done this. James 4:6, says, *"But He gives greater grace. Therefore it says, 'God opposes the proud, but gives grace to the humble.'"* Seek inner healing over any generational and bloodline pride, murderous words, word curses, etc.

Seek covenant with one another. Comparison cannot remain in the atmosphere of covenantal relationships. A full understanding of what covenant and covenant relationships are will help give us the tools to destroy the stronghold of comparison in our lives. Being in covenant one with another is a pride killer. We need covenantal relationships with our fellow believers, so pride and jealousy will not arise.

Each of us has been made unique and different from each other. That is what makes us so beautiful. Each of us is without rival in every way. Not one of us falls behind in any gift unless we choose to. We are fearfully and wonderfully made in His image (Psalm 139:14, Genesis 1:27). Once we come to the full realization of who we are in Him and who we are together, comparison will no longer be an area where the enemy can capture us.

Unteachable, Rebellious, and Unsubmitted

The child of pride is an unteachable, rebellious, and unsubmitted spirit. Having an unteachable spirit will prevent our discernment from being in full operation. An unteachable spirit says things like, *"Do not correct me," "What I am doing is just fine," "Well, so-and-so does it this way, and it works for them."* How about, *"They do not recognize nor honor my gifting"?* Each of these statements is a clear indicator of being unteachable, rebellious, and unsubmitted to authority. We have to keep ourselves in check at all times. When we are unteachable, we are operating in the spirit of rebellion and are what is termed *"stiff-necked."* 1 Samuel 15:23 (NLT) says, *"Rebellion is as sinful as witchcraft, and stubbornness as bad as worshiping idols..."*

Our hearts must remain in a place of teachability. No matter how keen my discernment is, I always submit to those who have the spiritual rule over me and learn from their wisdom and guidance. Never think you are the full authority of operating in any gift. There are others who God uses that are just as powerful in their gifting as you are in yours. When we are rebellious, we lose the anointing just as Saul did. The spirit of the Lord left him quietly even though he had been anointed and chosen by God to be the king of Israel. His disobedience to the word of the Lord through Samuel cost him everything.

The level to which we are submitted to the spiritual authority over us is the level of which our gifts will operate. Hebrews 13:17 tells us, *"Obey your leaders and submit to them, for they keep watch over your souls as ones who must give an account. Let them do this with joy and not with groaning, for that would be of no benefit to you."*

We grieve the spirit of those over us if we are not submitted to their authority. When our leadership sets out guidelines for us to operate safely in ministry, they do so for our benefit, not their own. When we are not submitted to the authority over us, we are bucking against God Himself. Romans 13:1-2 says, *"Let every person submit himself to the governing authorities.*

For there is no authority except from God, and those that exist are put in place by God. So whoever opposes the authority has resisted God's direction, and those who have resisted will bring judgment on themselves."

Submission brings freedom and honor. Skip Heitzig writes about this in his article for Decision Magazine:

"Most people think of freedom and submission as opposites: If you submit, you're giving up your freedom. But, by submitting in honor of God, you're gaining greater freedom. William Barclay said, 'Christian freedom does not mean being free to do as we like; it means being free to do as we ought.' In restricting certain freedoms, you gain others. You have the freedom to live your life in the open before others, to let it be on display and let them scrutinize you because you have nothing to be ashamed of; whatever accusations they bring against you won't stick."[4]

Even Jesus submitted to authority – in the Garden of Gethsemane and to those who arrested and tried him. He yet submitted to the cruelty of the cross. He knew, if He had not submitted, the devil would have a legal claim against Him. I have heard it time and time again that the devil is a legalist. When we are unteachable, rebellious, and unsubmitted, the enemy has a legal claim against us in the Courts of Heaven. This transgression gives him full authority to rob us of our God-given destinies and the ability to operate in our gifts and callings. It will strip the anointing from our lives.

The book *Undercover* by John Bevere speaks heavily on the subject of submission and is a strongly suggested read for greater understanding. We must understand the proper way to submit to authority whether or not leaders, bosses, or elected officials are Godly or ungodly.

If you find yourself in any of the above-listed scenarios, seek inner healing. There are many resources available through various ministries. Inner healing and deliverance cannot be done enough. It is through our healing and cleansing that we will be able to operate fully to the Glory of God the Father. Inner healing is nothing to be afraid of nor intimidated by. It is freedom. Galatians 5:1 says, *"It is for freedom that Christ has set us free. Stand firm, then, and do not let yourselves be burdened again by a yoke of slavery."* Yeshua paid for our freedom. It is up to us to seek after it as to obtain it.

Believing the Great Lie of Religion

Inner healing and deliverance is an element that the church as a whole has denied. They will lie to congregations and lull them into believing all is well once they get saved. The mainstream churches across America have really done a great disservice to their congregations by denying the need for further inner healing and personal deliverance.

I grew up in a very dogmatic denomination that believed that every curse was done away with at the cross, and we are no longer held responsible for any curse associated with any sin whatsoever. Most denominations believe this way. The error in this is a little thing called *"iniquity."* Iniquity can be defined as any willful and inner act of disobedience to God. It is having our way instead of God's way. It is those hidden sins. It deals with our actions and attitudes. William Merritt paints a very clear picture of the subject:

> *"Iniquity is a predisposition to certain strengths or weaknesses. It refers to the way you are 'bent.' One of the Hebrew words for iniquity is 'avon' which describes the crooked and perverse attitudes that emanate from the father to the children. An iniquity usually involves an attitude or behavior that is more entrenched than a sin. A synonym for iniquity is wickedness; other synonyms include evil, sin, vice, crime, injustice."*[5]

Merritt goes on to explain:

> *"Generational sins, curses, and patterns come to us through the attitudes,*

actions, beliefs, behaviors, and/or habits that we have inherited from our family or relatives. We then 'enter into' the same sin pattern and make it our own. It is usually repeated throughout our life as well as by individuals in successive generations."[5]

When we willfully sin, we open the door to the enemy granting him a legal right to our lives and that of our children and grandchildren. The consequences of repeated sin are transferred to us from our forefathers. Thanks, Adam. Scientific evidence is beginning to show that our DNA, our very genetic code, holds the collective memories of previous generations. Sin is part of those memories. Sin became part of our genetic makeup at the fall of man in the Garden of Eden.

When we fall into the same sins that our forefathers did, we are enabling the enemy to bring a curse upon us. The repercussions of the sins of our family lines become an active and very present reality. Once we are cleansed from sin at salvation, we still have to deal with the consequences of those sins. Our sins are our own, but the effects of those sins can last for generations. Take, for instance, a woman who is promiscuous and becomes pregnant. Upon her salvation, her pregnancy doesn't disappear. There are consequences to her sin. This is the same as a person who is a drug addict. After salvation, this person will still have to deal with drug cravings and damage done to his or her body by using those drugs.

So what are some examples of generational iniquities? Things such as anger, rage, abuse, abandonment, fear, idolatry, sexual sins, unbelief, low self-esteem and self-worth, pridefulness and jealousy are all generational iniquities. This list can go on and on and manifest in a wide variety of ways.

When I came out of witchcraft, I was led to believe that everything I had done was over and done. I walked out that lie for years thinking everything was cut off and finished. I was so wrong. The more I walked with the Lord, the more He brought things to my attention with which I needed to deal. As the Holy Spirit was working on me, things manifested. Yes, things were broken off and expelled as this happened. The deeper my walk with the Lord went, I was still tugged on in the spirit realm. I felt shame over my past and suffered from depression and suicidal thoughts. Rejection was a major fight for me. I struggled with it long after being saved and filled with the Holy Spirit. No one knew I was living in my own little private Hell. I was tormented continuously all the while the enemy bombarded me with accusations. Fellow Christians were no help as they too were struggling in secret with the same if not worse issues.

When I was introduced to true spiritual healing, then the changes came. The more I go through inner healing and deliverance, the deeper my walk is becoming. My worship has come alive. I do not go around bragging when I have inner healing and deliverance as this is a personal experience for me. There have been things dealt with in the privacy of inner healing that would cause most Christians to run and hide. The freedom I experience now in my walk is ever-increasing with each session and with each layer of renunciations I do. I am chasing my freedom and submitting to continual inner healing. I do not consider myself to have fully arrived, but this one thing I do – I forget what is behind and straining toward what is ahead of me (Philippians 3:13) to the best of my ability. Do I stumble? Yes, but I get up and go again. Will I miss it? Yes, and so will you. We keep pressing and moving forward through the pain and the tears, knowing that God has our backs. I will not give up on who God has called me to be. You shouldn't either.

If you need inner healing and deliverance, do not hesitate to reach out for help. Yes, there will be times the Lord will visit you and work with you one on one in the intimate seasons with Him. But, you should never only rely on that. God has placed people in our lives to help sharpen us and to facilitate our healing. You have to be willing to submit to it. Do not let anything keep you from your freedom. Get rid of every weight and entangling sin (iniquity) and run with endurance the race set before you (Hebrews 12:1).

Section 2

Next Level Discernment

Chapter Seven
Multidimensional Discernment

There is a component of discernment that has been misunderstood. Most people have chalked this type of discernment up as merely being *"prophetic."* Do not get me wrong; I am not discrediting prophetic revelation in any shape, form, or fashion. What I am referring to is what happens when the prophetic merges with the gift of discernment and becomes one – operating simultaneously.

This deep layer of discernment has been boxed in by religion and stripped away by the occult. With this level of discernment, someone can see into the spirit realm to a particular place at a given point in time. I call it *"Multidimensional Discernment."*

There is a component of discernment that has been misunderstood and mislabeled. Most people have chalked this type of discernment up as merely being *"prophetic."* Do not get me wrong; I am not discrediting prophetic revelation in any shape, form, or fashion. What I am referring to is what happens when the prophetic merges with the gift of discernment and becomes one – operating simultaneously.

This deep level of discernment has been boxed in by religion and stripped away by the occult. With this level of discernment, someone can see into the spirit realm to a particular place at a given point in time. They can see the possible outcomes of certain situations. I call it *"Multidimensional Discernment."*

With multidimensional discernment, one can accurately pinpoint what is in operation back to its point of origin. Those who have trained themselves in this type of discernment can easily discern something happening in the spirit realm at a different location, even if that location is hundreds of miles away. Or if that event occurred in the past. This information can bring insight into current situations. Now, do not base everything solely off discernment. If you sense a past event on a piece of property, do your due diligence to research and verify that event. If you are picking up something in a person's bloodline, gently let them know so they can investigate it. We honor never tear down.

We know there is neither time nor distance in the spirit realm, so seeing in this realm is part of our Godly spiritual inheritance. Through the Holy Spirit, we can see through the dimensions of time and space to discern events at their given place in history or even as they are happening.

We have scriptural references to multidimensional discernment in both the life of Yeshua and Paul, the Apostle. John 1:47-48 says, *"Yeshua saw Nathanael coming toward Him. He said, "Look, a true Israelite! There's nothing false in him." Nathanael said to Him, "How do you know me?" Yeshua answered, "Before Philip called you when you were under the fig tree, I saw you."*

In 1 Corinthians 5:3 (GNT), Paul states, *"For even though I am absent in body, yet I am with you in spirit, and I am glad as I see the resolute firmness with which you stand together in your faith in Christ."*

Paul could not have seen the believers at the Church at Corinth except through spiritual eyes, a.k.a discernment. The same with Jesus seeing Nathanael. We know that God is no respecter of persons (Acts 10:34). Everything the disciples walked in is available to us. All we need to do is ask and receive in faith. Jesus said that because He was going to the Father, we would do greater works than He did (John 14:12). God shows no partiality to anyone (Gal. 2:6). It stands to reason based on Scripture that we can, through the Holy Spirit, have our discernment strong enough to peer through the distances and sense the spirits in another location. It is a technique that will take much practice and honing.

The occult terminology for multidimensional discernment is *"Remote Viewing"* and *"Scrying."* By definition, Remote Viewing "is a mental faculty that allows a perceiver (or a *"viewer)* to describe or give details about a target that is inaccessible to normal senses due to distance, time, or shielding."[1]

When the occult uses remote viewing, they are looking through the dimensions of time and space to where something happened or might happen to see where events of today can affect the future. They are looking for a way to connect back to the past. Remote viewing is done by the occult using the *"third-eye"* and familiar spirits for selfish gain. Multidimensional discernment is done through the power of the Holy Spirit by a person whose sole purpose for discerning is for the glory of Father God and to see people healed.

The U.S. government has secret training centers for those who have a natural bend towards this type of discernment. If governmental systems are seeking out and training individuals who have a predisposition towards multidimensional discernment, how much more should the Church be doing the same? It is for us to operate in it proficiently.

"Scrying" is very similar to remote viewing. Scryers are seeking to tap into the unseen through the use of *"the in-born second sight"* (discernment in other words). Second sight is the ability to see things that cannot be easily perceived through our natural senses.

Scrying dates back to 10th-century Ancient Persia and is mentioned in a text called the "Shahnameh." When scrying, the scryer is staring into a reflective object such as a bowl of water, mirrors, or crystals. Native Americans used smoke to perform something very similar to scrying, while Ancient Egyptians used bowls of oil to scry.

This type of discernment allows practitioners to *"predict"* the future. What the occultist is actually seeing is the possible outcomes of a specific situation in a person's timeline. Each of these outcomes has a wide range of variables based on choices. Each choice has its own *"offshoot"* or *"branch"* on the timeline with its own set of variables and consequences for each subsequent decision. What the occult does is scan these variables and pinpoint the scariest outcome and pronounce that over a person to bring fear and extort money to prevent this negative outcome.

Think of these branches as guitar strings. The strings are all side-by-side on the guitar with a distinctive sound and a corresponding note. They are all strings, but different in thickness and note. Depending on which string you pluck will be the note you get. Each string resonates in the sound hole of the guitar creating an individual sound. Picking out which string you might choose to play and the corresponding note is precisely what soothsayers do.

Try this example. If you go left at the stoplight, you may miss the heavy traffic that is straight ahead. If you go right at the light, you may hit a pothole and have a wreck. It is all based on choice. What the occult does is scan these possible choices and crafts a compelling scenario that causes fear that motivates you to do anything to prevent the negative outcome. It's all about fear, control, and manipulation.

With multidimensional discernment, we as believers can discern the times and seasons we are living in and make accurate decisions based on the leading of the Holy Spirit. We can discern where to go to church and where to go to eat afterward. We can discern where God is moving and shift our schedules around so we can be a part of the action.

Multidimensional discernment can be a valuable tool in helping with deliverance and inner healing. With this type of discernment, a deliverance minister can accurately pinpoint when contracts were made to demonic entities in the bloodline of those receiving ministry. They can also pinpoint the source of occult influence over a person's ancestry that is causing issues in the present. They can even pinpoint the source of occult influence over a person's lineage that is causing problems in the present.

As co-heirs of Jesus Christ, we have the full authority to operate in this kind of discernment. It will take much prayer and practice to be able to see clearly into the spirit realm in this way. There isn't a 12-step program or a secret formula or power prayer to operate in multidimensional discernment. It will take practice and patience both. If you are willing to stretch your discernment to the max, then begin seeking deep intimacy with the Father and allow Him to open up this realm to you. This level of discernment is not for the faint of heart, though. If you are fearful about what you will experience, then do not go after this.

Practical Application 1:

In this training exercise, we will practice multidimensional discernment. Do not be upset if you are not able to operate in this type of discernment right away. It will come with practice and patience.

- ➢ Ask a trusted friend to write a message on a piece of paper and hide it in an odd place that you would never think to look.
- ➢ Allow a few days to pass, and ask the Father for clues about the message and its location.
- ➢ Once you have your clues, share to verify your information to see how accurate you were.
- ➢ Repeat the process by asking a different friend.

Practical Application 2:

This one will be much more difficult unless you are already operating in the prophetic. And it takes a great deal of trust between you and the other person for this one. Again, be patient and give yourself grace as you grow.

- ➢ Ask a trusted friend to allow you to discern their bloodline. It will help if your friend already has a good understanding of events in their bloodline.
- ➢ Pray for clues of timeframes, locations, and events.
- ➢ Write everything down and then present it to your friend for verification.
- ➢ Repeat the process with a different friend.

Practical Application 3:

In this exercise, you will be asked to discern where the Lord is moving and how to get to that location. It may take a few tries to get this one right, so give yourself grace. This exercise is a safe one to do by yourself.

➢ Enter into worship and a time of prayer.

➢ Ask the Father to show you a location where He is moving.

➢ Ask if you may join Him there. If He says *"yes,"* proceed to the next step. If the answer is *"no"* then praise Him anyway and call it a day. The key here is to be obedient.

➢ Ask Him for specific directions on how to get to the location. Follow every instruction the Father gives you to the letter.

➢ Once in your location, enjoy your time with your Heavenly Father. Ask questions as to why He is there and what He wants to accomplish. Protect what He tells you.

➢ Praise Him for allowing you to stretch your discernment.

Always remember to grant yourself grace as you are seeking to operate in more profound levels of discernment. Do not pressure yourself to get everything right every single time. You will miss things. I miss things. It is not your job to see, feel, and hear everything that is going on in the spirit realm. You are only responsible for what the Lord shows you. So breathe.

Chapter Eight
The Importance of Sound

This chapter has been the most difficult to write due to the spiritual attack that came with it. The more I attempted to write this chapter, the more I began to feel closed off and choked out. From frequent computer crashes to my worship falling short, I could not gain a breakthrough. The enemy did not want this one written. One of my dear friends felt that it had to do with my sound needing to be reset. After struggling for an entire day, I put everything down and took a break.

The next day, I woke up at 3:43 am. Now, I tend to take note of times and look up the corresponding Strong's Hebrew and Greek numbers to see if the Lord is speaking through the numbers. He was this day. The word entry at 343 in Hebrew means *"oppression, distress, and calamity."* The entry in the Greek for 343 means *"unveiling, uncovering, and take away."*

I submitted myself before the Lord and repented for my bloodline misusing sound. I asked the Father to retune me to His frequency and break all ungodly sound connections and frequencies. Immediately, I felt dizzy, and then the flood of the Holy Spirit washed over me. I grabbed my mini shofar and pointed the curved part towards my belly so that the sound would go into there, and blew. I, then, proceeded to repent for any wrong sound released by the former owners of our property and us into the land. I asked for a frequency reset for both the land and my home. I blew the shofar again and felt something break loose in the spirit realm. I was then able to breakthrough with praise and dancing before the Lord.

What is Sound?

Dictionary.com defines sound as *"vibration or disturbance that travel through any medium by transferring energy from one particle to another and can be heard when it reaches a person's or animal's ear."* Sound exists as pressure waves, called *"sound waves,"* sent through a medium (gas, solid, liquid) to a receiver. These waves move longitudinal (or lengthways) through liquids and gases, but travel both transverse (across) and lengthways of the particles through a solid.

The measurement for sound is called *"decibels."* A decibel is a degree of loudness. The speed of sound in dry air is 343 meters per second, which means it will travel one mile in about five seconds. Sound will travel four times faster in water and twelve times faster through steel. When a plane goes faster than the speed of sound, it ruptures the sound barrier causing what we know as a sonic boom. The ensuing boom happens when the sounds waves are forced together at a high rate of speed.

Sound waves cause these medium particles to vibrate and collide with one another. This is the reason why there is no sound in a vacuum seeing that in a vacuum, no particles exist that can interact with the sound waves. Sound waves are carried or moved along by the particles within the medium. Irregular repeating sound waves create noise, while regular recurrent waves produce musical notes.

Sound waves are characterized by frequency, duration, amplitude, and wavelength. Frequency is the number of vibrations of the medium particle per second. There are two types of frequencies – low and high. Low refers to the bass sound, and high refers to the tenor sound. These two exist together creating a dimension to the sound we hear.

The duration or time period of a sound wave refers to the amount of time taken by the medium particle to complete the vibration. Duration is inversely proportional to frequency. Amplitude is how loudly the sound is received. Wavelength is the amount of distance the sound wave has traveled through the medium.

When two sounds waves come together, *"superposition"* occurs. Superposition is when two waves occupy the same point at the same time. Superposition creates interference. Interference can occur in two forms – constructive and destructive. In constructive interference, the two waves complement each other amplifying their sound. In other words, they co-exist in perfect harmony with one another. The low and high waves flow together up and down at the same place. In destructive interference, the high and low points on each wave touch effectively canceling each other out. This principle is how noise-canceling headphones work. By releasing a sound with the opposite amplitude as the incoming sound, the two waves destructively interfere and thus cancel each other out. And, no amplitude is released.

Both of these phenomena can happen within the same superposition. When two waves of similar frequency arrive at the same point and superpose, they alternate with constructive and destructive interference. The resulting superposition produces a pulsing known as a beat. The pulsing beat will rise and fall in amplitude as the wave travels.

When sound waves reflect off a surface, it creates an echo. This echo creation is what is termed *"sound reflection."* Echoes are usually a single burst of sound and a clear reflection of the originating sound. We experience delays between when a sound is released and its corresponding echo due to the time it takes the reflected wave to return. The farther the distance from the originating source of sound is, the longer the delay will be in the reflected sound. Echos can be used to distinguish the distances of objects in a space. Sound reflection is used by sonar and ultrasound equipment to create recognizable maps of the ocean floor or the human body respectfully.

Similar to the echo is *"reverberation."* The brain perceives reverberation as one continuous sound. We usually experience reverberation in closed spaces such as an auditorium with multiple reflecting surfaces or objects. This effect is created when a large number of reflections of sound build up and then are absorbed by the objects in the room, causing the sound to decay.

Sound waves change across the medium they travel when diffraction and refraction occur. Diffraction happens when the waves are traveling across a medium at a constant speed hits an obstacle causing the sound waves to bend across the barrier. This is why you can be in one room down the hallway of your home and a radio in an adjacent room, and you still hear it. Refraction happens when the speed of the sound wave changes as it moves across from medium to medium.

Another sound phenomenon is called the *"Doppler Effect."* Doppler effect is a change in frequency and wavelength of a wave caused by the change in distance between the thing creating the wave and what is receiving it. For example, you hear an ambulance approaching. The sound starts off low, but the closer it gets to you, the louder the sound becomes. As it passes you, the sound recedes becoming softer.

Shifting Sounds

In the beginning, God spoke, releasing sound, and created everything. All of creation releases a reflection of that sound. The Bible says in Psalm 19 that the heavens themselves declare the glory of the Lord. Psalm 19:3-5 says, *"Day to day they speak, night to night they reveal knowledge. There is no speech, no words, where their voice goes unheard. Their voice has gone out to all the earth and their words to the end of the world."*

All the heavenly bodies (planets, stars, constellations, etc.) speak. Their voice carries throughout the known universe and beyond. It all sings with the sound of the One who created it. It sings back to Him His song of creation. The energy is measurable and echoes throughout the known universe. Science has proven the stars and planets release recordable sounds. NASA has spent a great many years of recording, researching, and analyzing these sounds. You can listen online to the sounds of the planets and our sun on their website.

Nikola Tesla once said, *"If you want to find the secrets of the universe, think in terms of energy, frequency, and vibration."*

Russian Occultist Helena Blavatski understood the principle of sound and frequency. She wrote in her paper *"Hierarchies:"*

> *"In the eternal music of the spheres we find the perfect scale corresponding to the colours, and in the number, determined by the vibrations of colour and sound, [and] which "underlies every form and guides every sound," we find the summing-up of the Manifested Universe."*[1]

Every part of creation releases a very similar sound that harmonizes with each other. For instance, whale songs when sped up by fourteen times sounds strikingly similar to bird songs. Music is a reflection of the harmony Yeshua designed for the Body of Christ to mirror as we are fitly joined together (Ephesians 4:16). Each of us believers carries our own personal sound God placed in us that harmonizes when we are in unity with our fellow believers into a gorgeous refrain in which the Father takes delight. In essence, we sound like Him when we come together in unity.

When God sets us in place, and we are operating in that place, our portion of the symphony is played. Orchestras contain four sections – strings, woodwinds, brass, percussion. Each section has its own hierarchy – first, second, and third chair. First Chair is a position of distinction, chosen by the conductor, that will usually go to a highly competent player, although not necessarily the best player of the section. The first chair leads the section, giving the rest of the section their cues and direction on inflection, dynamics, bowings, etc. They set everyone else in tune. The first chair also recognizes the potential within fellow players in their respective sections, and grants solo parts, and raises up those players. Hmm...resembles the Biblical model for the church, but I digress.

All occult activity is based on the release of sound, whether it is chanting and vocal resonance, drumming, or the ringing of bells. Every aspect of spell casting involves sound. The occult uses sound to capture the hearts of people. They will also use sound to reach *"ascension."* Ascension is *"rising or increasing to higher levels, values, or degrees."* The occult attempts ascension by playing sounds that are first soothing to relax the mind and body, then follow those with higher frequencies based on the first sounds. As the frequency and tones change, the higher the practitioner ascends in the spirit realm.

Our bodies respond to specific frequencies and harmonics, bringing healing or worsening our conditions based on those frequencies and harmonics. Science is finally catching on to the use of sound in healing.

During the 1920s, a physician named Royal Raymond Rife experimented with sound and healing. Rife discovered that viruses and bacteria vibrated at a specific frequency and could be destroyed by using a different frequency. Think of how opera singers can change the frequency of voices to match the frequency being emitted by a glass, causing it to shatter. Doctors Sadeghi and Sami write about Rife on their website:

> *"Rife discovered that a simple electromagnetic wave wasn't enough to destroy a microorganism. Instead, he found the body readily accepted a radio frequency wave if it was emitted by gas within a glass tube. This allowed the frequency wave to penetrate deeply into the body with scalpel-like precision. Because the wave was precisely tuned to the frequency of the microorganism, only the pathogen was affected, leaving the surrounding tissue unharmed."*[2]

Rife ended up recognizing the frequencies of and curing, anthrax, cholera, tetanus, B. coli, influenza, spinal meningitis, tuberculosis, pneumonia, syphilis, gonorrhea, leprosy, streptococcus, conjunctivitis, bubonic plague, staphylococcus, diphtheria, typhoid, and a variety of cancers. The medical community discredited him; his work confiscated and destroyed. He died in poverty. Now science is proving his research by verifying the body heals with the use of sound.

The indigenous peoples of the world have used sound for centuries. Sound chambers have been discovered in Egypt, Australia, Malta, and in Central and South America. Tibetan monks use their voices and brass bowls to heal and enter into trance-like states for meditation. Dr. Mitchel Gaynor, Director of Medical Oncology and Integrative Medicine at the Strang-Cornell Cancer Prevention Center in New York, has conducted various studies of the Tibetan *"singing"* bowls and the sound they produce. He has discovered these bowls resonate at a frequency that soothes the nerves, calms fear, and boosts the immune system. Gaynor also discovered quartz bowls to have a much more direct impact as they can be tuned into any note.

Gaynor states in an interview:

> *"Whether it's the Sufis and their chants, or the Tibetan Buddhist chants, or the mantras used in yoga or the Gregorian chants sung at Vespers, or prayers from the Jewish Kabbalah....where they believe that every vowel sound is a divine sound... all of these...even the African ritual chants and Native American songs and chants use virtually identical tones and sounds to elicit a deep meditative state. So, it doesn't require believing in any dogma. These sounds affect us on a physiological, spiritual, and emotional level."*[3]

Hitler used sound as a means of controlling the masses. Nature releases sound at 432 Hz. All of the music was being written and performed at 432 Hz. Hitler brought an entire country under his influence by changing the frequency of the music of that day from 432Hz to 440Hz. The result was marked increases in depression or hopelessness, fear, aggression, and oppression.

However, the first use of 440 Hz was not done by Hitler at all. In 1885, the Music Commission of the Italian Government declared that all instruments and orchestras should use a tuning fork that vibrated at 440 Hz. The American Federation of Musicians accepted the 440

Hz as the standard pitch in 1917 thus backing the Italian shift. The US conducted many experiments on the use of 440Hz. These experiments showed music could provide an effective form of crowd control, and could also fulfill a military objective.

During the 1940s, the United States introduced the 440Hz standard worldwide and was accepted by the International Standards Organization in 1953 as the standard for musical pitch, thus forever changing our music. 440Hz has been referred to by many who study it as *"The Devil's Interval."* In a paper titled *"Music Cult Control,"* Dr. Leonard Horowitz wrote, *"The music industry features this imposed frequency that is 'herding' populations into greater aggression, psycho social agitation, and emotional distress predisposing people to physical illness."*[4]

We see a vast majority of people walking around with earbud in listening to music written in a frequency that goes against our God-given frequency. Mind-control has been achieved. How does the occult use this? Satanic music is full-throttle at 440Hz. Oddly enough, however, the majority of music used in Wicca, Shamanism, and Druidism is at 432Hz.

432Hz is God's standard for the universe. The planets, stars, all of nature (including us) resonates at 432Hz. Nature-based occult follows this same standard. I firmly believe this is part of the allure of such practices. It draws people based on the sound in which our bodies were meant to resonate. The occult will release sounds in this frequency to mesmerize people and draw them to the occult. As our bodies respond to the sounds being released, we will naturally be captivated. By the use of sound, parts of our body can react and change its function. Sound waves can cause our heart to slow down and signal for us to go into sleep mode. Oh, that we would take back our sound for the Kingdom!

The Solfeggio Frequencies

There have been six tonal frequencies rediscovered that are believed to make up sacred music, including the Gregorian chants. These tones make up the *"Solfeggio Frequencies."* The word *"solfeggio"* refers to a vocal exercise in which the sol-fa syllables are used. Supposedly, these tones, when sung in perfect harmony, impart spiritual blessings to the singer and hearer. Each of these frequencies is believed to be comprised of a frequency required to balance your energy and keep your body, mind, and spirit in perfect harmony. Solfeggio tones were introduced by Dr. Joseph Puleo and Dr. Leonard Horowitz in the 1970s. These two physicians and herbalists discovered six electromagnetic sound frequencies in an ascending six tone scale that corresponded to the syllables from the hymn of St. John the Baptist. The original scale was developed by an eleventh-century music theorist named Guido d'Arezzo. The six-scale sounds were taken from the first stanza of each line of the hymn – ut, re, mi, fa, sol, and la. The hymn of John the Baptist looks like this in Latin:

*Ut queant laxis **Re**sonare fibris*

*Mira gestorum **Fa**muli tuorum*

*Solve polluti **La**bii reatum*

Sancte Iohannes

The literal translation of the hymn is *"In order that the slaves might resonate (resound) the miracles (wonders) of your creations with loosened (expanded) vocal cords. Wash the guilt from (our) polluted lip. Saint John."*

The main six Solfeggio frequencies are:

➢ **396 Hz** – Liberating Guilt and Fear

➢ **417 Hz** – Undoing Situations and Facilitating Change

➢ **528 Hz** – Transformation and Miracles (DNA Repair)

➢ **639 Hz** – Connecting/Relationships

➢ **741 Hz** – Expression/Solutions

➢ **852 Hz** – Returning to Spiritual Order

Today, these names are still in use in musical notation – do, **re**, **mi**, **fa**, **sol**, **la**, ti, do. Octave by octave, the precise frequency associations measured are derived from a particular musical temperament; however, the frequencies Drs. Puleo and Horowitz used are different as they were generated from the Book of Numbers in the Bible, *"using a Pythagorean reduction algorithm based on our decimal number representation, applied to verse numbers 12 through 83 of chapter seven."*[5]

Nikola Tesla once said, *"If you only knew the magnificence of the 3, 6 and 9, then you would hold a key to the universe."* The fundamental root vibrations of Solfeggio Frequencies consist of the numbers of 3, 6, and 9. These numbers also correspond to the fractals Arthur Burk speaks of in some of his teachings. Each fractal corresponds with our spiritual walk and our physical bodies. These frequencies shift us back to our original design.

Harmonic Circles

There is a rarely understood principle that is part of music theory but has occult applications. It is called Harmonic Circles. It is also called *"Circle of Fourths, Circle of Fifths,* and *"Cycle of Fifths."* Basically, the Circle of Fifths is a representation of all 12 notes in the chromatic scale, arranged into a circle. It's most commonly used to easily find the notes in any major or minor key." This tool can also give the student of music theory a solid intuition of chord progressions. This tool has life applications when finding the ideal place for music and harmony to reside. Each note will build off another, progressively creating larger and larger circles around the central circle as the musical composition is built, layer upon layer. The circle begins to spiral as it expands and begins to resemble the shell of a Nautilus.

How is this used in the occult? Notice there are 12 tones in total. There are also 12 Zodiac, months in a year, colors on a color wheel, and 12 chakras – seven in the physical body and five that relate to how a person connects to the universe (supposedly). Sacred geometry fits neatly inside the Circle of Fifths.

If you can layout the Circle of Fifths over a clock face, A is at 12 o'clock. Each subsequent note follows the face of the clock all the way around – E = 1, B = 2, F# = 3, C# = 4, G# = 5, D# = 6, A# = 7, F = 8, C = 9, G = 10, and D = 11 (# represents the sharp). Divide the octaves into three equal parts, and you get an augmented chord. The formation of this division forms a triangle that is referred to as *"The Devil's Door."* Splitting the triangle in half will divide the octave into four minor thirds. The triangle itself divides the octave into three equal major thirds. This stacking results in a very scary-sounding chord.

Harmonic Resonance

"Harmonics" and *"resonance"* are integral components of sound. Harmonics refers to an overtone accompanying a fundamental tone at a fixed interval, produced by the vibration of a string, a column of air, etc. in an exact fraction of its length. Resonance, on the other hand, refers to the quality in a sound of being deep, full, and reverberating. Harmonics refers to the natural frequency of a musical instrument, while resonance is the cause of sound production in musical instruments.

The occult maps out the *"harmonic resonance"* of a location based on harmonic circles. Harmonic resonance is defined as *"an extraordinarily diverse and varied phenomenon seen in countless forms throughout the universe, from gravitational orbital resonances to electromagnetic oscillations, to acoustical vibrations in solids, liquids, and gases, to laser resonance in light and microwaves."*[6]

Harmonic resonance will cause a piece of crystal to sing, and musical instruments to play in response to a specific note or sound from another instrument. People in close proximity will have their heartbeats synchronize. Clock pendulums in a shop swing together in unison. This point of synchronization is what the occult is looking for. It is the optimal place for unity in spell work.

Every community, city, state, and nation has a harmonic circle from which all harmonic resonance for that area emanates. It will set the entire tone for that place to operate in unity. If a harmonic circle has been disrupted or moved, there will be chaos. This chaos will include, but not limited to, political unrest, emotional uneasiness, violence, governmental corruption and upheaval, poverty, and premature death.

Scientists are beginning to study the manipulation of the harmonic resonances and how it affects insects. Results of testing have yielded some fascinating results. Experiments have shown bugs will behave differently to their environment when the harmonic resonance changes. For instance, a millipede can be manipulated into not using all of its legs to walk. Manipulation of the harmonic resonances of individual people has been suggested to create nightmares, hallucinations, violent behaviors, muscle spasms, and ultimately changes the thinking patterns of entire groups of people. The shift is such a subtle one that we humans do not even realize we are being manipulated.

There is a Biblical example of changing the harmonic resonance of an area. It is found in the 37th chapter of Ezekiel. The Lord carries Ezekiel to a valley of dry bones and tells him to prophesy that the bones would live. Ezekiel prophesied, and the bones came alive. Ezekiel changed the harmonic resonance of the valley to match that of the Father. Ezekiel spoke from his place of authority in the Father and spoke life. The bones had no choice but to respond!

Recovering Our Sound

The occult has taken information about sound and resonance and contorted it so much that the church no longer accepts this type of teaching. It is labeled as *"New Age," "woo-woo," and "demonic."* The use of sound has been ever since God spoke all of creation into existence. The nothingness responded to the frequency of His voice, and out of it, everything was formed. God's sound released the energy necessary to create matter from anti-matter.

When we receive a negative doctor's report about our health, are we countering it with the Word of God, or are we rehearsing with our family and friends the negative sound released over us? To what sound is your body responding? Go back to the interferences we discussed earlier in this chapter. When the positive Word of God hits the negative words of the enemy about us, destructive interference happens. One cancels the other. If we agree with the lies of the enemy, constructive interference occurs, and the sound is reinforced.

Science has proven that the release of sound can heal or destroy. How have we released our sound? The group Switchfoot recently released a new song that has really grabbed my attention, and now I know why. The song is all about releasing the right sound. The song says, *"show me the place where your words come from."*[7] From where are your words coming? Our words are our song. From where is our sound emanating? It is from the overflow of the heart the mouth speaks (Matthew 12:34). Our sound is released from the depth of our hearts.

The song goes on to say, *"Love is the language; love is your native tongue."*[7] Our sound was always meant to be love. Not just any love, but the love of the Father. That perfect love we read about in 1 John 4:18. The lyric that caught me the most was *"My friend, where did we go wrong? My Lord, we forgot our sound."*[7] We have indeed forgotten our true sound. We cut people down with our words trapping them in emotional hurts and wounds.

92

The song ends with these phrases, *"I want the world to sing in her native tongue; To sing it like when we were young; Back before the pendulum had swung to the shadows; I want the world to sing in her native tongue; Maybe we could learn to sing along; To find a way to use our lungs for love and not the shadows."* [7] Wow! Wow! Wow!

Proverbs 18:21 says, *"Death and life are in the control of the tongue. Those who indulge in it will eat its fruit."* What sounds are we releasing into creation? Are we subduing creation with the Word of God, or are we subduing it with words of anger, malice, hate, corruption?

May our hearts be rent asunder over the wrong sound we have released! Repentance, true Godly repentance, mixed with Godly sorry retunes our hearts to the Father's. Proper alignment with our apostolic covering, inner healing, and deliverance, honoring those in leadership, praying for each other, walking in the perfect love of the Father with one another all play a role in keeping us in tune. Take some time to do an inventory of yourself. Listen to the sound you are releasing. Are you critical; are you complaining; are you always in a huff? Or are you releasing blessings over others? Are you calling out the best in others? Are you praying for, not about, those who ridicule and belittle you? Your words will reveal your sound.

If you find yourself hit by any of this, then repent to the Father for allowing your sound to be corrupted by the cares of life and the weight of the world. Seek inner healing to help retune you. Ask the Father for revelation concerning your sound.

Practical Application 1:

This exercise may be a bit strange at first and possibly out of your comfort zone. You may do this exercise alone in the comfort of your own home. Turn off all distractions before you begin. Your focus here is on the Father.

➢ Enter into a time of prayer and intimate worship of the Father.

➢ Open up your heart to Him and ask the Holy Spirit to reveal the areas in your life where you are releasing the wrong sound, and repent.

➢ Ask the Father to reset your sound.

➢ Offer up praise to the Father and enjoy His presence as He ministers to you.

➢ Set an appointment and keep that appointment with a qualified deliverance and inner healing minister for deeper cleansing.

Practical Application 2:

In this exercise, you will be discerning the sound of your home. You can actually do this one by yourself.

➢ Enter into a time of prayer and intimate worship of the Father.

➢ Become very still and quiet, then ask the Father to hear the sound of your home and if it needs to be reset. If He tells you that the sound needs to be reset, Ask the Father for strategies for resetting the sound. Follow the leading of the Holy Spirit and obey the instructions that the Father gives you.

➢ Thank the Father for walking with you through this new dimension of discernment.

➢ Once you have done what the Lord has instructed, have someone you trust discern the sound of your home again to ensure it has been set correctly.

Practical Application 3:

For this exercise, you will be discerning the harmonic resonance of your city or town, and write a report to give to your area leader. Please make sure you have a discernment buddy. The best place for this is outdoors in a public park.

➢ Pray and ask Yeshua to show you where in your city you need to go to discern.

➢ Pray and worship en route to the location the Holy Spirit reveals to you.

➢ Once on-site, listen carefully to the ambient sounds, i.e., birds, traffic, people's voices. You are listening for anything that sounds off or echoey.

➢ Begin to pray and ask the Father to allow you to discern the harmonic resonance of the city. What sounds do you hear in the spirit? What sensations do you feel as you listen?

➢ Ask the Father if someone has tampered with the harmonic resonance of your city. Take notes on what He reveals, but do not take anything on. Remember, this is a recon mission only, not a prayer journey.

➢ Thank the Father for the experience and knowledge you have gained from your growing discernment.

➢ Leave the area and debrief with your discernment buddy.

➢ Submit a written report of your findings to your area leader so a prayer strategy can be formed.

Chapter Nine
Portals, Gates, and Altars

We have heard the terms *"portal"* and *"altar"* thrown about within Christian circles from time to time. Some believe it is a false doctrine to teach on the existence of heavenly and demonic gates or spiritual openings in the earth. Others dwell too heavily on them and go from experience to experience with portals and angelic openings without a clear understanding of what is the real purpose of these openings. Using scriptural references, I will try to shed some light on this subject matter, as well as discuss what an *"altar"* is and how it relates to portals.

Portals and Gates

The definition of a *"portal"* is an opening between the natural and the supernatural. They are direct access points to the divine or the demonic. God designed portals for Heaven to touch Earth. Dr. Patti Amsden defines portals as *"points where heaven and earth converge."*[1] A Godly portal will act as a conduit for provision, transportation/translation, and revelation.

There is an argument among many Christians about whether or not portals are scriptural. Are portals in the Bible? Some believe portals exist based on experience while others believe they do not exist because they are not in the Bible and therefore only of the devil. The problem is not whether or not portals are mentioned in the Bible. The problem is with semantics. *"Semantics"* is defined as *"the branch of linguistics and logic concerned with meaning."* The Bible does imply the existence of portals. Now, the Bible does not come right out and use the word *"portal."* Instead, the words used are *"gates"* and *"doors."*

Psalm 24:7 states, *"Lift up your heads, O **gates**, and be lifted up, you everlasting **doors**: that the King of glory may come in"* (emphasis mine). The word used for *"gates"* is the Hebrew word *"sha'ar,"* which means *"gate of entrance to a court, palace, temple, court of the tabernacle; heaven."* The word used for doors is the Hebrew word *"pethach,"* which means "opening; such as a door or gate; entryway; opening place." The Merriam-Webster dictionary defines a portal as *"a door; entrance; the approach or entrance to a bridge."* So there you go. A portal is a door, and a door is a portal.

This information leads us to another question. If gates are entrances and doors are entrances, are they then the same thing? No, they are not. In the above verse, we see that the Bible makes a distinct separation between the two. Paul Cox and Barbara Kain Parker write about this in their book Exploring Heavenly Places, Volume 3 - Gates, Doors, and the Grid. They state, *"a gate is an entrance to a dimension, and within a dimension are many doors...the key is the doors, and the doors must be opened in order for the gates to remain open."*[2]

Think of it this way. You have a fence around your property with a gate at the driveway. You have a door on your house. The gate at the driveway is not the entrance to your home. The gate is the entrance to your domain, and the door is the entrance to your palace.

1 Kings chapter 19 refers to Mt. Horeb (some translations list this location as Sinai) where God revealed Himself to Elijah. We find the first mention of Mt. Horeb in Exodus chapter 3 with Moses and the burning bush. It is also where Moses struck the rock and water gushed out, providing for the people. It is also at Horeb that God revealed His glory to Moses and cut a covenant with Israel giving them the Ten Commandments. Mt. Horeb is a portal in which our Heavenly Father met with the prophets of old. Jerusalem is also one of the oldest and largest portals known to man.

Our role with portals is to protect and steward the portals and gates of our home, city, region, state, and nation. We are to be watchmen and gatekeepers over these portals. Proverbs 8:34 gives us a glimpse of this, *"Blessed is the one who listens to me, watching daily at my gates, waiting at my doorposts."* Here the word *"gates"* is *"deleth"* meaning a door or gate;

97

doors of Heaven. It also references something that swings like a valve of a door. *"Posts"* in this verse is *"mĕzuwzah"* means where the hinges are or doorposts. It is from the same root as *"ziyz"* meaning fullness and abundance. The word *"doors"* again is *"pethach"* as in Psalm 24:7.

Good Portals Can Go Bad

God places portals on the Earth at His discretion for His glory. When we fail to do our job as watchman and gatekeepers, the enemy can shift the portals into the demonic. The occult/demonic can stop the flow coming from the Third Heaven and only allow things from the Second Heaven to pass to Earth. Those who practice witchcraft can build altars in or around the portal and perform rituals causing the portal to align with darkness.

Unfortunately, Christians can open ungodly portals in an attempt to open a Godly portal. This occurrence happens when we are operating in wrong motives, under the influence of demonic spirits, having an uncleansed bloodline, and flirting with the occult, i.e., Pokémon, Ouija Boards, horoscopes, visiting psychics, etc. Most Christians who open ungodly portals are entirely unaware they are opening the wrong type of portal. We must be very, very careful when we are desiring to open portals to make sure we are operating in the correct spirit.

As Christians, we do have the ability to open Godly portals. Again, it is at God's discretion that portals open. All we need to do is ask and create an altar of pure worship to our Father. Just remember, God opens portals at His discretion. John 14:14 says, *"If you ask Me anything in My name, I will do it."* Psalm 118:19-20 states, *"Open to me the gates of righteousness, that I may enter through them and praise Adonai. This is the gate of Adonai— the righteous will enter through it."*

Before opening a portal check yourself! James 4:3 (AMP) issues this warning, *"You ask [God for something] and do not receive it, because you ask with wrong motives [out of selfishness or with an unrighteous agenda], so that [when you get what you want] you may spend it on your [hedonistic] desires."* It is crucial that you check your motives to make sure you desire the portal for the right reasons. Follow the guidance of the Holy Spirit as to the purpose of your portal. You must also be prepared to defend and steward the portal. If you are not willing to pay the price, ***DO NOT OPEN A PORTAL!***

Portals Can Occur Anywhere

Portals can occur in almost any place where altars have been built and dedicated. Man-made objects like paintings, mirrors, windows, light fixtures, doors and fountains, holy and sacred sites, cemeteries and burial mounds are prime locations for portals as well as natural places such as between two trees or in a grove of trees, high places, waterfalls, and caves.

Sometimes portals will come in pairs. Always look for a secondary portal where there are large active portals. An example would be an open death portal and a deity portal open within proximity. A death portal is a demonic portal open for the sole purpose of causing the death of people (usually at random) who pass into the portal at just the right time. The occult opens these portals through rituals involving blood sacrifices. A deity portal is a demonic portal open due to another portal giving a principality a legal right to have access to the area. I encountered this once at the site of an old plantation home while on a team prayer assignment. A death portal was close to where the old plantation home once stood with a deity portal was at the entrance of the property. Always deal with the first portal. The deity portal will usually close on its own once the central portal is closed. Remove the legal right, and the deity portal will collapse on itself

Gatekeepers and Watchmen

All portals will have a gate and a gatekeeper. The gatekeeper's job is to allow things to pass in and out of the portal, to hide the portal from others, and control the activity of the portal. A watchman's job is to protect the interests of the portal and to alert the entity who created it by sounding the alarm of approaching danger to the gatekeeper. Godly portals can have both gatekeepers and watchmen as well. They are usually angelic, but that role can fall to us as well. We are to be both watchmen and gatekeepers of the portals in our assigned areas.

Ley-lines and Portals

A ley-line is a line of electromagnetic energy flowing over and through the Earth in both horizontal and vertical lines. They were put there by God. We know them as lines of latitude and longitude. The foot traffic of our ancestors also created ley-lines as they traveled to and from sacred sites as discovered by Alfred Watkins in the 1920s. Ley lines can also be attached to graves of people leading back to their home sites.

The occult can create ley lines by giving another person an item/object that has a spell or curse attached to it granting the occultist access to that person or placing an object at one location and attaching a spell to a different location.

The occult will attach ley-lines to portals via spell casting. This act is done through astral projection, physically at the portal or by placing a talisman or device in or at the portal opening. The occult will attach ley-lines to portals via spell casting. This act is done through astral projection, physically at the portal, or by placing a talisman or device in or at the portal opening. A talisman or device, as defined by Dictionary.com, is *"a stone, ring, or other object, engraved with figures or characters supposed to possess occult powers and worn as an amulet or charm."*

Placing a ley line in a portal allows the occultist access to the portal without having to be physically at the portal. Portals can also be opened on the intersection of ley lines to increase their power.

Closing a Demonic Portal

<u>NEVER SHUT A MAJOR PORTAL ALONE!!!!!</u> Always have someone with you. You will ALWAYS need backup.

- ➤ Cover yourself and your team in prayer first and foremost.
- ➤ Listen to the guidance of the Holy Spirit and obey the will of the Father concerning the portal. ALWAYS start with repentance.
- ➤ Determine if there is a ley line attached to the portal, deal with the ley line first. If not, then someone can reopen the portal.
- ➤ Send back anything demonic back through the portal first. You do not want any critters running around loose. Invite the Hosts of Heaven to come and assist in the removal of any entity that has come through the portal. Once you sense that everything has gone back through, follow the prompting of the Holy Spirit on how to proceed.
- ➤ Find the gate and the gatekeeper if there is one. Send the gatekeeper through the portal
- ➤ Address the portal first and command it to close in the name of Yeshua.
- ➤ Address the gate and command it to close in the name of Yeshua. Sometimes, the Father will send an angel to sit in the gate, and you do not have to do anything more at that point. If this happens, it usually means He has a purpose for the gate which He will have you address at a later time.
- ➤ Ask the Hosts of Heaven to come chain both shut with the lock of the Holy Spirit.
- ➤ You can also release sound into the portal. It can be a worship song or just a sound.

Portal Realignment

It might be the will of the Father to realign the portal, especially if He told you the portal

101

needs to stay. Only realign if the Father says the portal is to remain on the land. Do not just realign because you think you have the authority to do so.

> ➢ Cover yourself and the team in prayer before continuing.

> ➢ ALWAYS start with repentance.

> ➢ Ask the Father if He wants the portal to remain open. If He says yes, then press on. Don't argue. If He says not to touch it, then listen and obey.

> ➢ Determine if there is a ley line attached to the portal, deal with the ley line first. If not, the occult can easily realign the portal back to the darkness.

> ➢ Command any entity that has come through back into the portal from whence it came and ask the help of the Hosts of Heaven.

> ➢ Find the gate and gatekeeper if there is one.

> ➢ Send the gatekeeper through the portal.

> ➢ Ask the Father to send an angelic gatekeeper to set a guard at the gate.

> ➢ Command the portal to realign in the name of Yeshua.

> ➢ You can also release sound into the portal. It can be a worship song or just a sound.

Yeshua is a Living Portal/Door

Yeshua is himself a living portal. Yeshua states in John 14:1, *"Yeshua said to him, 'I am the way, the truth, and the life! No one comes to the Father except through Me.'"* Ephesians 2:18 (AMP) goes on to say, *"For it is through Him that we both have a [direct] way of approach in one Spirit to the Father."* Ephesians 3:12 tells us we have access to come boldly to the Father through Yeshua. He is our point of entry to the 3rd Heaven so that we can have direct access to God, the Father.

With Christ within us, we now have an active portal within us. Just as with God's holy portals releasing His holiness and glory upon the Earth, our inner portal or door releases the holiness of God and His glory within us. We, in turn, bring that to the land. 1 Corinthians 3:16 (NLV) tells us, *"Don't you realize that all of you together are the temple of God and that the Spirit of God lives in you?"*

The word *"temple"* in this verse is *"naos,"* meaning a sacred edifice consisting of the Holy Place and the Holy of Holies. The original tabernacle and the temple were portals to Heaven. Now, through Jesus, we are the temple and tabernacle of God.

Jesus is our inner God door/portal dwelling within our spirit man. It is our spiritual Holy of Holies. It is where the very power of God resides within us. This connectedness is recorded in scripture. 1 Corinthians 6:17 states, *"But the one who joins himself to the Lord is one spirit with Him."* John 7:38 (AMP) says, *"He who believes in Me [who adheres to, trusts in, and relies on Me], as the Scripture has said, 'From his innermost being will flow continually rivers of living water.'"*

Our spirits are portals or wells for the divinity of Christ to flow out and into those around us. The occult fully understands this concept. The knowledge of our inner God dimension has been stolen and perverted by the occult. Many false religions refer to it as the *"god or goddess within," "inner flame," "inner flow,"* or *"the 10th gate."*

103

Altars

Now that we have established that portals exist and what they are, how are they opened? Portals are opened by altars, whether created in the natural or in the spirit. What exactly is an *"altar"*? We have heard this term in ministry settings to refer to a place of repentance or worship in the church building, usually at the front of the sanctuary. This terminology is, in essence, an accurate description. An altar is a place of sacrifice. An *"altar"* is the meeting place of two dimensions. Altars can either be a blessing to the land or bring a curse. Demonic altars and portals stop spiritual revival and cause social decay while God's holy portals open the holiness of Heaven upon the Earth.

Dr. Patti Amsden writes the following about altars in her book *Portals: Releasing the Power and Presence of God into the Earth*,

> *"Altars have attendants in both spheres (earthly and spiritual). The agent to raised the earthly altar functions as a priest or gatekeeper to keep the portal open. The deity to whom the altar was dedicated becomes the supervising spirit or gatekeeper to the spirit's domain."[3]*

Whatever deity the altar is dedicated to is who controls the portal. The altars act as gateways to allow traffic between the spiritual and physical realm to move through a portal. Whoever controls the gates by way of the altars controls the traffic between the dimensions.

At occultic altars, the practitioners will do rituals, release sound, cast spells, and offer sacrifices to their chosen deity or demon. God can supersede the altar entirely and open a portal because, well, because He's God. Christians can open heavenly portals with the key of pure worship. It is the sacrifice of worship offered up that unlocks the heavenly realm creating a portal to the throne of God.

The Altar of our God Gateway

Our hearts are the altars of our God Gateway. Yeshua has given us direct access to God, the Father, while the Holy Spirit is our gatekeeper or supervising Spirit. Is it any wonder King Solomon gave such a strong warning in Proverbs 4:23 when he said, *"guard your heart with all diligence, for it is a wellspring of life."* The word *"heart"* is more accurately translated as *"soul or seat of appetites."* Our soul, in other words.

It is at the altar, the place of sacrifice, that we die daily. 1 Corinthians 15:31 states, *"I die every day—yes, as surely as the boast in you, brothers and sisters, which I have in Messiah Yeshua our Lord."*

The word for *"die"* in this verse denotes the violent death of man or animals. It's a sacrifice.

An altar is a place of sacrifice. We die daily to our desires and fleshly appetites upon our inner altars as we give up our selfishness for His righteousness. Whatever we build an altar to within our hearts and begin to worship will open up a demonic door within us whether we want it to or not.

If we allow our inner portal/well to become defiled, it will realign to something else. God's portal within us begins to shut down. Our well dries up. Sadly, this is barely even noticeable to the one who is defiled. A false Jesus becomes the doorway to the demonic. How does this happen?

To understand this, we have to go back to ancient military tactics. Taken from Wikipedia:

> *"Well-poisoning is the act of malicious manipulation of potable water resources in order to cause illness or death or to deny an opponent access to freshwater resources. Well-poisoning has been historically documented as a strategy during wartime since antiquity and was used both offensively (as a terror tactic to disrupt and depopulate a target area) and defensively (as a scorched earth tactic to deny an invading army sources of clean water). Rotting corpses (both animal*

and human) thrown down wells were the most common implementation; in one of
the earliest examples of biological warfare, corpses known to have died from
common transmissible diseases of the Pre-Modern era such as bubonic plague or
tuberculosis were especially favored for well-poisoning."[4]

In the modern-era, poisoning the well has a new meaning. It revolves around the information we are feeding on. Wikipedia has this to say about poisoning the well:

"Poisoning the well (or attempting to poison the well) is a type of informal
logical fallacy (mistaken belief, especially one based on unsound argument)
where irrelevant adverse information about a target is preemptively presented to
an audience, with the intention of discrediting or ridiculing something that the
target person is about to say."[5]

In a nutshell, poisoning the well is slander. Call it smear tactics or defamation of character. We see this played out in our current political climate. We see it in our churches when ministries go after one another. It is allowing the Absalom spirit to take root in your heart and operate through us.

The enemy would love nothing more than to poison our well, so we can infect those around us and corrupt our church, ministry, relationships, etc. As the poison within us cultivates, we spread it to whom we come in contact.

Most of us think we could never do anything like this. What about our secret sins? The ones we don't want anyone to find out about: various addictions, negativity, pride, bitterness, hatred towards another, criticism, gossip, jealousy. All of these bring the strongmen in to control our inner portal defiling us without us knowing what has happened. Our well has become poisoned, and it begins to seep into the wells of others.

God's portal or door He placed in us is designed to bring His Glory to Earth, and His power

106

is made manifest. Likewise, the demonic releases its power through us when we defile our portal. This principal the occult knows all too well. Once the demonic has control, even just a little bit, of our portal or well, it will begin to influence all whom we come in contact. According to Dr. Patti Amsden, anyone who dwells under a portal created by an altar will be affected by the deity to whom the altar was dedicated. She goes on to say, *"the rank of the deity and degree of the covenant determine the parameters of the altar's influence."*[6]

If we are honoring God at the altar of our hearts, then those we are around will be influenced by God the Father. If we are honoring our flesh at our altars, then the works of the flesh will influence those around us as well. We need only look at scripture to see this played out. Abraham built an altar to the Lord in Bethel long before his grandson, Jacob, would lay his head upon a stone there. Jacob came under the influence of the Godly altar built there. The same was true with the people of Israel when the priests allowed demonic altars to be built in the land. The more demonic influence came into Israel, the more the people rebelled against God.

Jesus said in Matthew 12:34, *"Out of the abundance of the heart the mouth speaks."* If you want to know what is in your well or what your inner portal has aligned to, pay attention to what is coming out of your mouth. Go back and review the section on Blockages to Discernment in the previous chapter for more insight on your inner well-poisoning.

Practical Application 1:

Gates and portals will be different to you as you discern them. Discerning the differences of both will become easier the more you discern them. As your discernment grows, you may begin to feel a difference in portals. This shift happens as you begin to discern the age of the portal as well as the deity the portal is aligned. Pay close attention to what you are feeling. Does it feel familiar to anything you have felt before? Cross-reference your journal. If it is an unfamiliar sensation, make a note of it. The more you pay attention to your cues, the easier it will become to process your information.

In this exercise, you will discern a Godly portal and gate as well as determine the age of each. You will also be discerning whether or not the gate has a gatekeeper. Grab a discernment buddy and give this a try. Remember, no two people will discern the same way.

- Always cover yourself in prayer first and enter into worship.
- Ask Yeshua to reveal portals to you and pay attention to how your body reacts or what you see. Trust what you are sensing. Journal your experience so you can refer back to it.
- Look for natural formations that would lend themselves to a portal, i.e., circles of oaks, pairs of trees standing alone, doorways, light fixtures.
- Observe doorways, paintings, mirrors, etc.
- Look for markings on the ground or trees.
- Ask the Father to allow you to feel a Godly portal. Note the size and shape.
- Ask to discern a Godly gate and its gatekeeper. Take descriptive notes of what the gate and its gatekeeper look like.
- Ask to discern the age of the portal and gate.
- Praise Him for allowing you to stretch your discernment in this way.

Practical Application 2:

108

In this exercise, you will discern an ungodly portal, gate, gatekeeper, altar as well as determine the age of both the portal and gate. You will also be discerning whether or not the gate has a gatekeeper. I suggest doing this in a location away from your personal property for now.

➢ Always cover yourself in prayer first and enter into worship. Close off anything in your bloodline before continuing.

➢ Ask the Father to allow you to feel an ungodly portal feels. Note the size and shape and how your body reacts.

➢ Discern the altar that is allowing the portal to stay open.

➢ What type of altar is it? Is the altar in the physical or in the spirit?

➢ Ask to discern an ungodly gate. Take descriptive notes about how the gate and its keeper look.

➢ Ask to discern the gatekeeper.

● Is the gatekeeper a spirit or a human?

● Do your best to see if you can discern the way the gatekeeper looks.

➢ Ask to discern the age of the portal and gate.

➢ Discern if there are any ley-lines attached to the portal.

➢ Praise Him for allowing you to stretch your discernment in this way.

Chapter Ten
Seeing Through the Dark Curtain

There is a dark curtain over our world that many cannot see nor have the wisdom to combat. This dark curtain was skillfully woven by the enemy and strategically placed over all the inhabitance of the Earth when Adam and Eve fell. This curtain is the occultic activity. Not all forms of the occult are the same. It may seem like they should all be lumped together as one banner flag of *"witchcraft,"* but each branch of the occult functions differently than the other. Each branch has its specific deity or lack thereof. In this chapter, we will look at a few various elements of witchcraft and the occult.

I hope to enlighten you on what witchcraft is, and what the tools of the trade are to help better understand their tactics. Each form should cause a different reaction as you discern it. I feel pure witchcraft differently than I do Wicca, Druidism, and Egyptian Witchcraft. It will take practice to recognize how each form affects you fully.

What I have included for you here may seem laborious, but it is pertinent information for you to take and construct prayer strategies to cover yourself, your families, finances, and ministries to which you are connected.

What is Witchcraft?

Traditionally, witchcraft is the craft from the Old World and is often called *"The Old Craft"* and sometimes *"The Old Religion."* Forms of witchcraft date back as far back as ancient Egypt. Witchcraft can be defined as *"the practice of magic, especially black magic; the use of spells."* It is said that witchcraft is one of the oldest spiritual traditions in the known world. Witchcraft encompasses many different types of activities, including astrology, divination, spell casting, spirit communication, and demonology. It includes the practices of

110

many nations, cultures, religions, and many books and writings from ancient times. This form of the occult predates Wicca and can include many satanic practices as well as Luciferian and Gnostic elements. We are currently seeing a rise in those claiming to be *"Christian witches"* who claim the Bible is a book of sorcery.

Witches who practice traditional witchcraft may belong to any religion or none, they may believe in a god or gods, or they may be atheists. However, the majority of witches do honor and worship the goddess Hecate, also spelled Hekate . She is considered the goddess of magic, witchcraft, the night, moon, guardian of the household, protector of everything newly born, ghosts, and necromancy. Her name means *"worker from afar."* She is usually depicted as a *"hag"* or an old witch stirring a cauldron. Two familiars are associated with Hecate – a black female dog and a polecat or skunk. Hecate was often depicted in triple form as a goddess of crossroads. Her worshippers believe that she can see in three directions at once – past, present, and future.

Witches keep their spells, incantations, rituals, and secrets in a what is called a *"Book of Shadows"* or a *"Grimoire."* It is, in essence, their prayer journal. A witch's grimoire becomes part of them as they imbue it with their energy. Some Grimoires are passed down from generation to generation. The grimoires are also usually written in code called the *"Theban Script,"* *"Alphabet of Honorius"* or *"Witches Alphabet."* These alphabets and symbols bear striking resemblances to the written communication of modern gangs.

There are many branches of witchcraft called *"traditions."* Each tradition has its own set of guidelines and beliefs as well as alignments to specific deities, demons, and spirits. Some traditions of witchcraft are rooted in nature worship such as Wicca and Druidism, while others are rooted in the worship of stars and planets. It is important to note that witchcraft is not considered to be a religion, but more of a spiritual walk. Some religions incorporate witchcraft into their religious rituals such as Kabbalah, Santeria, Satanism, Voodoo, etc.

There are various tools used in witchcraft. A few examples are tarot cards, crystals, gazing balls, herbs, salt, grains, various animal and bug parts, dice, runes, casting bones, drums, cymbals, incense, candles, etc. There is a very long list with which I will not bore you. Witches incorporate various techniques in their practices such as casting circles, calling the quarters, various binding spells, etc. When one method looses its power or stops working, practitioners will shift to a different technique or even a different tradition to accomplish their goals.

If you have ever been personally involved in witchcraft, seek deliverance and inner healing. The practice of witchcraft invites demonic access into your life. Ask for renunciations for witchcraft, Hecate, and goddess worship. Ask the Lord if there is any generational witchcraft that needs to be broken. If so, schedule an inner healing and deliverance session with a trained minister.

One way we, as Christians, can personally combat any witchcraft coming against us is to make sure we are spiritually purifying ourselves daily. We can also increase our praise and worship, Bible study, and prayer life. Never underestimate the power of a prayer soaked life.

New Age and Universalism

"New Age" is not a religion, but a philosophy. It is defined as *"a broad movement characterized by alternative approaches to traditional Western culture, with interest in spirituality, mysticism, holism, and environmentalism."* This movement began in the 1970s as a breaking away from Christian *"narrow-mindedness."* It's roots, however, can be traced as far back to Medieval astrology, alchemy, Hermeticism, and in 18th-century mysticism pioneered by the likes of Emanuel Swedenborg and Franz Mesmer. New Age also exhibits the influences of Aleister Crowley's Thelema. This philosophy has given rise to the popularity of Wicca, witchcraft, and pagan religions. New Age philosophy teaches a *"holistic worldview"* in that there is oneness with each other and that believers will begin to see themselves emerge as gods.

It is within the confines of New Age that the false doctrine of *"Universalism"* was birthed. Universalism is the belief that all humankind will eventually be saved no matter whatever doctrine they follow. This doctrine pushes the *"co-exist"* mentality in that all religions lead to God. It also teaches all religions follow the same God. Universalists believe their chosen path to God is a spiritual and personal one, and no one path is greater than another. This belief also teaches there is no punishment for sin after death nor any singular savior of humanity.

New Agers tend to be easily recognizable with their crystals hanging from their necks; however, Universalists are not so easy to spot. They can speak *"Christianese"* rather effectively and tend to be highly charismatic. They teach grace, grace, grace. They teach that no one has to repent for their sins. It has a great draw to the younger generation who are fed up with religious rules and dogma. Universalism is also called Christian Liberalism.

If you have ever been involved in New Age or Universalism, repent. Ask a deliverance minister to help you with renunciations for New Age philosophies. Also, ask the Father for a shift in your thinking.

Covens

Witches can operate alone but are way more powerful within a coven. The Merriam-Webster dictionary defines the word *"coven"* as *"a collection of individuals with similar interests or activities; an assembly or band of witches."* The first recorded use of the word occurs circa 1520. The word "coven" is derived from the Middle English word *"covin"* with its meaning of *"agreement, confederacy"*, from Anglo-French *"covine"*, from Medieval Latin *"convenium"* meaning *"agreement,"* and from the Latin term *"convenire"* which means *"to agree"* and is the same root for the word *"covenant."*

The occult knows the power of unity. In their covens, witches operate out of pure agreement with a united cause. Any amount of disunity can cause one to be asked to leave the

113

coven or circle of fellowship. Witches will seek unity at all costs in the coven. They know that power flows through each member of the coven and connects each individual into a collective. They honor one another. Somehow, witches operate in the Biblical principle of Ephesians 2:3 which states, *"Do nothing out of selfishness or conceit, but with humility consider others as more important than yourselves."*

The bonds of unity are extremely strong in covens. They will sacrifice much for unity. Unity does not mean coven members never disagree. In their disagreement, they still honor each other. They never bring accusation publicly with any coven member. It is always handled member to member unless the matter cannot be resolved. Then, the issue is handed over the head of the coven to help resolve.

It does not matter to a witch if someone else within the coven is asked to perform a specific ritual. They all share the benefits of each member's skills and techniques. Their desire for unity knows no bounds. If someone steps out of unity, they are asked only to observe rituals and not participate as disunity will cause the ritual to fail. Each person in the coven is viewed as valuable and has their own gifts and callings that bring wholeness to every group.

Within a coven, there is trust and community. Covens are formed to provide a safe place for each member to practice freely with one another as they share themselves freely with one another. Coven members share in each other's energy and harness it for the common good of the group. If one member lacks, the other members come to their aid. There is a flow between each member of love and harmony. If one member hurts, they all hurt with the one. When a member is rejoicing, the entire coven celebrates. Sounds a lot like Romans 12:15 does it not?

Sexual exploration and enjoyment between members are encouraged as it brings tighter unity. The coven view on sex between members is that it is for recreation and sharing of energies. This bond creates a more vibrant environment for trust and mutual love within the coven. They will also blur the lines of gender and be more fluid in their sexuality.

The occult is quick to identify each individual's gifts and catapult those individuals into operating in those gifts. Once an individual's particular skill set is identified, they are trained by a mentor for a specific degree of the coven. This placement will be that person's role for the entire time they are part of the circle. Covens can consist of varying degrees and hierarchy. Those who are more proficient in the craft will have a *"coven within a coven"* meaning those particular practitioners will operate in a smaller more specific coven geared towards their skill set as well as serving in the larger coven. There are teaching and training covens for initiates (those just coming into witchcraft), avid learners, and for anyone interested in learning the craft. Each level of teaching covens is designed to help hone the skills of the members so they can take their proper place in the coven and even one day set them on the path to creating their own coven if they so choose.

Covens can consist of only three members and up to as many as twenty. Although covens consisting of sixty or more are not unheard of. There are no gender or cultural biases within covens, however, there are gender and culture-specific covens. Everyone is welcome, even those who are given more to the darker side of the craft. It takes all to create the balance needed to bring harmony to the coven.

Covens will also join forces with other covens to bring about the desired effect. If a coven is having difficulty with a powerful Christian disrupting their spells and hold over an area, they will join a more powerful coven to bring an end to the threat. They will even join forces across traditions, meaning they will join with other covens who practice a different tradition than they. We are currently seeing this in our rather strange political climate. We have a wide variety of witchcraft and occult traditions coming together in perfect unity to cast spells against politicians.

Covens are a perverted version of our prayer circles, churches and apostolic centers, and Bible study groups. We gather under the covering of the Almighty. If we gather together in true unity and the fellowship of love, no coven can ever stand against us. When we are in perfect unity advancing the Kingdom of God, we become what the occult terms *"nasty Christians."* Let's turn the enemy on his ear by seeking unity with each other even if it means laying down our pride and our agendas. If we seek after unity, we are fulfilling the prayers of Yeshua that we be one as He and the Father are one (John 17:20-21). Remember, unity takes time and effort on the part all participants involved. Unity does not mean we become doormats either. Unity creates an atmosphere where we can share and be open without fear of judgment from others.

Practical Application 1:

In this exercise, you will be asking the Lord to be able to discern pure witchcraft. This may take some time to adjust to. Some feel it immediately, while others take some adjusting to discern it accurately. Remember, the more you are in the presence of the Father, the easier it will be to sense the works of the enemy in comparison. Again, no distractions.

➤ Meet with your discernment buddy and pray about a place to discern. Keep in mind that this is discernment ONLY. You are not to take on a witch or a coven, nor any principalities in the area.

➤ Ask intercessors to cover you as you discern.

➤ Once the location has been chosen, cover yourselves in prayer and worship in route.

➤ Upon arrival, walk around the area and look for visual clues that witches have been there, i.e., markings on the ground or trees, objects that are out of place for this area.

➤ Become still and ask the Father to allow you to discern any witchcraft that may be in the location.

➤ Ask if there are any covens in operation in the area.

➤ Take notes on how your body begins to react. Are you feeling emotions? Do you smell something strange? Do you have pains or pressures in your body? Record everything.

➤ Once you have a good idea of how witchcraft feels, leave the location.

➤ Pray as you leave to knock off anything that could be there set up as a watcher.

➤ Enter into a time of praise and gratitude to the Father for the experience and the stretching of your discernment.

➤ **CHALLENGE:** Do this exercise again in a place where there may be distractions such as a park full of children playing or lots of road noise. Take notes on how having distractions change your discernment.

Wicca

Wicca and traditional witchcraft may look identical at times, but there are subtle differences. At one time, Wicca was nothing more than the flower children enjoying the *"high life."* There are a lot of modern witches who claim they are Wicca and that their religion has been around longer than any other. This belief is incorrect. Wicca did not start until sometime in the early twentieth century in England. Wicca became popularized in the 1950s by Gerald Gardner and spread to the United States during the 1960s. Some speculate Wicca was birthed from Druidism due to their love of nature and a desire to be in harmony with it. Wicca follows a strict code of conduct called *"The Wiccan Rede,"* which states, *"Do what thou wilst, but do no harm."*

Wiccans view of magic is that it is a law of nature and not anything supernatural. Wiccans sometimes deny the existence of black magic, and some are opposed to spell casting of any kind. Spell casting within Wicca is always benign, and they will not harm even someone who wants to harm them. Like Christians, they turn the other cheek and leave revenge to karma. Typically, they believe it is morally wrong to interfere with the free will of another.

Wicca is a religion whose adherents are alternatively called Wiccans and *"witches"* (even though not all Wiccans practice witchcraft). Wiccans generally acknowledge and revere a pantheon of gods and goddesses as they draw upon a diverse set of ancient pagan and 20th-century hermetic motifs for its theological structure and ritual practices. They celebrate cycles with both the moon and the sun. Even though Wicca displays Celtic influences, it is not Celtic in origin or nature.

Wicca is typically duo-theistic, worshipping a god and goddess, referred to as the *"Lord and Lady."* The god is called *"the Great Horned God,"* and the goddess is called *"the Moon Goddess."* Dianic Wicca is a tradition of Wicca that only honors the goddess and only allows females into their covens.

The Wiccan goddess is called *"Triple Goddess"* who embodies all stages of a woman's life – maiden, mother, crone. The triple goddess consists of Demeter, Persephone, and Hecate. Each stage has a corresponding moon phase waxing, full, and waning respectfully. The symbol of the Wiccan goddess is a circle with two opposite facing crescent moons on either side and can be depicted with a pentagram in the center of the circle. The upside-down horn pendants on modern jewelry is a Wiccan symbol for their goddess.

Wicca teaches all life is sacred and needs to be revered. Some have characterized Wicca as being one of the most life-affirming religions. As with many religions, Wicca holds to a belief in the five elements – earth, fire, air, water, and spirit. Each element is a living and conscious entity with which one can partner.

Druidism

Druidism, also called *"Druidry,"* is a religion that was taught by Druids. It is a nature-based religion just as Wicca and New Age are, but with a focus on ancestry and nature. There is no religious dogma or set sacred texts and therefore, can take on many forms. Those who practice Druidry can be pantheists, polytheists, monotheists, and animists. Druidry emphasizes the spiritual nature of life.

The main elements of druidic belief are the sacredness of all life, the Otherworld, reincarnation, nature, healing, journey, potential, and magic. Druidism practices tolerance of many different philosophical and spiritual traditions and teaches that no one system of thought is more authentic than any other.

Druidic Casts: Bards, Ovates, and Druids

Within ancient Druidism, there were three general casts – Bards, Ovates, and Druid. Each of these casts carried our different tribal tasks for each clan. Some see to the affairs of more than one clan.

The bards would keep the history of the clans alive in song and music. It is recorded that in Ireland the bards would train for 12 years to learn grammar, hundreds of stories, poems, philosophy, the Ogham tree-alphabet. The Ogham tree-alphabet is an ancient alphabet used from about the 3rd century A.D. to write Old Irish and other Brythonic/Brittonic languages which includes languages such as Pictish and Welsh.

The ovates were the native healers of the clans who understood the healing power of herbs. They were also the undertakers. The ovates specialized in divination, conversing with the ancestors (necromancy), and prophesying the future.

The druid cast was the professional class in Celtic society. They functioned as priests, teachers, ambassadors, astronomers, genealogists, philosophers, musicians, theologians, scientists, poets, and judges. Some sources say the druid class underwent 20 years of training. Druids presided over all public rituals, which were generally held within groves of sacred trees. In their role as priests, they acted not as mediators between the gods and man, but as directors of ritual, as shamans guiding and containing the rites. The word "druid" itself is an old Celtic word meaning *"knowing or finding the oak tree."* The earliest known mention of druids appeared in the 3rd century B.C.

Trees and the Druid

Trees are very sacred to the Druid. They represent life and knowledge and are revered as the keepers of the ancient wisdom. There are six sacred trees to the Druid believers – Oak, Ash, and Yew, followed by the Apple, Elm, Linden and Cedar trees.

Druids view trees as keepers of knowledge and ancient wisdom. A wealth of information is believed to be held by the tree and available for the Druid to tap. Trees, especially Oak trees, are revered in the Druid religion as keepers of the past and keepers of deep magic. The use trees to gain knowledge of where portals, ley lines, and other covens are. Not only will they obtain information, but they also gather Earth energies for strength and healing. Dark druids will release spells into tree to activate curses in the land against Christians as a whole. The majority of druids will not do this unless you are a direct threat to them by bringing their members to Christ or trespassing on their sacred ground. Faithful Druids respect all religions and will not go after someone just because that person is Christian. Only dark druids will do such an act.

Post-Modern Druidry

Druidism has evolved over the centuries. In the early part of the twentieth century, George Watson MacGregor Reid began the Church of Universal Bond in Britain which promoted socialism. During the late 1940s to early 1950s, this church evolved into The Ancient Druid Order under the guidance of Ross Nichols and Gerald Gardner, the founder of Wicca. In 1963, The Reformed Druids of North America (RDNA) was formed in protest to Carlton College's mandatory Sunday church service. After Gardner's death and the death of MacGregor Reid's son (who was the Druid chief) in 1964, Nichols formed The Order of Bards Ovates and Druids (OBOD). RDNA folded but left its mark. The American Druid Foundation (ADF) was established off the teachings of the RDNA. Both the ADF and OBOD are among the growing religions, as many are leaving Christianity for the old religions.

Practical Application 2:

In this exercise, you will be asking the Father to allow you to discern Wicca and Druidism. Doing this will take some practice as it may affect you similarly as pure witchcraft. DO NOT do this alone. As with the majority of our exercises, you need someone with you during this application exercise. Remember, no distractions.

➢ Chose a place to discern. Remember, this will not be a prayer journey, just discernment. You are not taking on any principality, strongman, nor practitioner.

➢ Cover yourselves in prayer and enter into worship on the way to the site.

➢ Ask the Father to allow you to sense how Wicca feels to you. Take notes on smells, sensations, emotions, etc. as you discern. Also note how Wicca feels as compared to witchcraft.

➢ Ask the Father to allow you to sense Druidism. Take note on how different this feels than Wicca and witchcraft. Take note on smells, sensations, pain, or temperature changes.

➢ Thank the Father for allowing you to stretch your discernment and praise Him for the experience.

➢ Worship Yeshua as you leave the site.

Necromancy

We have all seen advertisements or shows about people who speak to those who have passed from this life. I am sure many people would love to hear that their loved ones made it to heaven or that their loved ones are watching over them. The practice is called Necromancy. Merriam-Webster's dictionary defines Necromancy as *"conjuration of the spirits of the dead for purposes of magically revealing the future or influencing the course of events."*

In ancient times, practitioners of Necromancy would live near or in graveyards, mutilate the dead, sometimes eat flesh from the corpse, and wear the clothing from the deceased person to be able to draw the spirit from the dead. To summon the dead, practitioners stand over the grave of a particular person or lay on the grave with candles in hand, staring up at the stars to enter into a trance-like state. Others will take the dirt from atop the grave or chip a piece of stone from the tombstone.

Medieval practices of Necromancy followed a specific ritual set. All rituals were done at midnight. If the weather was stormy, then it was believed to be the perfect condition to conjure the dead. A coffin of the intended person to resurrected would be dug up and opened. The body was then removed and laid in a crucifix position with the head facing east. A dish of mixed wine, mastic, and sweet oil would be lit and placed near the right hand of the body. Practitioners believed this would aid in conjuring the deceased's spirit. Incantations were recited based on a practitioners tradition. The focus of the incantations and spells was on commanding the spirit to move in the name of the deceased person and answer the demands of the living.

If everything went as planned, the body of the dead person would slowly rise. If the spirit cooperated by answered the questions posed by the necromancer, it would be promised future peace. After the spirit was sent back to where ever it came from, the body would be burned so that it would not reanimate again.

123

Practices of Necromancy have varied from region to region; however, the most practices used the lighting torches to help create an eery backdrop of morbidity. Some practitioners would enter the cemetery and draw magic circles around the grave and burn plants believed to contain power such as hemlock, sage, aloe, opium, and mandrakes to aid in their conjuring.

The Catholic church has always condemned Necromancy even though they practice it with relics of the body parts of long-dead saints. Taking bones, teeth, blood, hearts and other organs, the Catholic church would pray over those items and proclaim that anyone who touched the relics would receive power, protection, and revelation from the dead saint. This practice is what Necromancy seeks to do.

There is a variety of occultic religions that still practice Necromancy today. Voodoo, Quibanda, Umbanda, Macumba, Santeria, and Freemasonry all practice some form of Necromancy. The occult uses Necromancy today to attract those who are longing for divine revelation of the future, the power to perform, seeking to win an election, etc. to capture the participants into a cycle of dependency upon the practitioner. The unsuspecting seeker does not realize they are communing with demons. Out of their desperation, they are blinded to the truth. Often, the seeker will become a practitioner themselves under the tutelage of a more experienced practitioner. Modern-day Necromancy is more prevalent than one might think. Practitioners teach rituals for seekers to speak to the dead for themselves and how to channel their influence, power, and insight. We see people flocking to events such as John Edward's Crossing Over in hopes of having a loved one reach out to them from the beyond. These practices are strictly forbidden in scripture.

Deuteronomy 18:10-11 (AMP) says,

> *"There shall not be found among you anyone who makes his son or daughter*
> *pass through the fire [as a sacrifice], one who uses divination and fortune-*
> *telling, one who practices witchcraft, or one who interprets omens, or a sorcerer,*

124

or one who casts a charm or spell, or a medium, or a spiritist, or a necromancer [who seeks the dead]".

We know that wisdom and insight about our future should always come from God the Father. The dead cannot speak to us from beyond the grave. The dead have no power over or in our lives. The only influence we have from the dead is the example they lived. We learn lessons from that person's lifestyle and choices.

Mediums are not consulting with loved ones. They are consulting with familiar spirits and demons. We have the authority to silence the mouths of these entities to prevent them from speaking to anyone. If you hear of someone coming to your city doing this, begin to pray against the familiar spirits from speaking. Bind up all spirits of death, manipulation, mesmerization, and divination. Release the Spirit of God's Revelation, the Spirit of Life, the Spirit of Truth to operate in your area.

If you have consulted mediums to speak to a dead loved one or have practiced this sin yourself, please quickly repent of this. If the Lord reveals to you that your ancestors practiced Necromancy, seek inner healing and deliverance to break the generational pull, sin, and curses that occur from ancestral Necromancy.

In this exercise, you will be asking to experience what it feels like when Necromancy has been done at a location. **DO NOT** do this alone.

- ➢ Enter into a time of prayer and worship, making sure to close any generational doors of Necromancy.

- ➢ Ask the Lord for a location to go and discern Necromancy. Pray and worship en route.

- ➢ Once on-site, look around carefully and pay close attention to any strange things on the ground. Are there any unusual smells?

- ➢ Ask the Father to allow you to feel what Necromancy feels like in the spirit.

- ➢ Ask the Father to discern if any entities have been summoned and are still in the location. Take notes on what He tells you.

- ➢ Thank the Father for the experience you have gained during this time of discernment.

- ➢ As you leave, pray that nothing can follow you out or attach to you. If the Lord permits you to, bind all entities to the location so they may not leave.

Casting Circles

Casting Circles are one of the most basic of practices for witches. This practice spans a variety of witchcraft traditions and cultures. The purpose of a circle is to create a sacred, magical space where the witch is able to meditate or perform a spell, healing, or a ritual of protection or gratitude. In actuality, the circle is more of a sphere. Like a protective bubble for those who are doing spell work. It is a place to offer worship and to practice the craft safely. The walls are constructed of pure energy and prevent anything from entering or exiting the safety of the walls. Within this bubble, there is no time nor place. The practitioner is between the worlds when inside the circle. It is, in essence, a portal from which the witch can access the spirit realm and commune with their chosen spirit deity.

126

Casting circles can be either in the spirit realm or the natural. Usually, when a witch casts the circle, they do so with their finger in the air in a large circular motion to create the circle around them. When in the natural realm, a witch will draw the circle on the ground. They can use salt, chalk, stones, and draw in the dirt or paint the ground to create the circle. Candles can surround a physical casting circle. The candles are usually on the outside edge of the circle in North, East, South, and West locations; however, the candles can be placed all around the circle. The circle can contain symbols related to the practitioner's tradition. Usually, the pentagram will be in the middle of Wiccan casting circles. In Native American traditions, a symbol relating to their particular deity or spirit guide can be drawn inside the circle.

Casting circles are being incorporated into floor tile designs in a variety of buildings in the modern era. The real purpose of these circle designs is currently unknown. There are two in the floor tiles on the first floor of the Mississippi War Memorial Building in Jackson, and several are on the floor of the Natchez Convention Center. There is a permanent casting circle with a fire pit in the center built in Madison County at the recreational area of a little tucked away subdivision. It is an area well-known for its witchcraft activity.

We know the enemy can only imitate the things of God. So, what would the Christian origin of casting circles be? When true manifest sons of God gather together in unity in prayer, that is our Godly example of what casting circles were meant to be. As we gather in a circle in the united bond of faith, fellowship, and prayer, we create an atmosphere in which the enemy cannot operate. John Ramirez discusses this in his book *Unmasking the Devil*. He writes about his experience against what he terms *"nasty Christians"* while practicing the craft for the enemy. This group of Christians chased his astral form from an entire neighborhood and rendered him powerless in that area due to their prayers.[1] This is what the Lord intended for *"casting circles"* to be – a place from which we cast out the enemy and render him powerless.

Calling the Quarters

In many witchcraft traditions, each element is assigned a direction. Those directions are called quarters. They are also called corners, watchtowers, and elementals based on various traditions. The quarters are usually called from North, East, South, and West (clockwise or *"deosil,"* also called sun-wise); however there are some traditions that will call in reverse or *"widdershin,"* which means counterclockwise. It is important to note that calling the quarters and locking the quarters of an area are NOT the same thing. Calling the quarters is *"Old World"* magic and is not regularly used by newer witchcraft traditions. Locking the corners of an area is to place that area under the dominion of a witch or coven of witches.

The quarters are assigned as follows: North – Earth, East – Air, South – Fire, West – Water. The occult views these elementals as lesser beings meaning they are not worshipped as a god or goddess. The elementals are ruled over by Lords of the Watchtowers, the Mighty Ones, and the Guardians. Some traditions recognize the quarters as living entities. The most well known are the gnomes (Earth), the undines (water), the sylphs (air) and the salamanders (fire). Those who honor angelic beings believe there are archangels associated with the four directions and their corresponding elements Uriel (North/Earth), Raphael (East/Air), Michael (South/Fire), and Gabriel (West/Water). Other practitioners, who follow Enochian and Golden-Dawn, call upon the *"watchtowers"* and believe the quarters are angelic beings that are to be summoned using elemental weapons and the names of God to gain their cooperation to guard the circle against (presumably) demonic interference. For some, the quarters are a metaphor of self with each quarter - earth correlates to the body, air to the intellect, fire to inspiration and water to emotion. Other traditions treat the quarters as pure, non-conscious energy that flows through all living things. Each tradition will call upon their own set of spirits for calling the quarters. When calling upon the elemental entities, there are a required specific set of ceremonial protocols to follow.

Each of the elements is also associated with a magical tool or tools. These tools also vary from tradition to tradition. The elements are also represented on many tarot card decks. Here are some general correspondences:

➢ Pentacle is Earth, and often considered a female principle.

➢ The wand or staff is Air (for some, it is the sword or athame) and is considered a male principle.

➢ Fire is the sword or athame (for some, it will be the wand or staff) and is considered to be a male principle.

➢ Water is represented by the cup, chalice or cauldron and is considered to be a female principle.

➢ The cauldron or pentagram can also represent the combination, integration, and mastering of the four elements.

Witchcraft traditions teach the purpose for calling the quarters is to center one within the cosmos. It is, in essence, calling upon the watchmen to bring all of your scattered pieces home and bring in the energy the practitioner needs for the upcoming ritual. By calling the quarters, all following rituals are grounded in the natural world. It is a foundation to build other rituals upon. The methods of calling will depend on the tradition of the witch. As the quarters are invoked, some traditions will use sound to seal the quarters while others will light a candle placed on the cardinal points. At the end of all the ceremonies and rituals, the quarters are then released from the circle. When the occult calls the quarters, it is an attempt to manipulate the elements into their control and effectively control others. Upon invoking these elemental entities, practitioners are inviting demonic entities to come and partner with them to gain power and control. Without realizing it, practitioners are giving away parts of themselves to these evil entities and become slaves to them. Any violation of the agreements made between the practitioner and the entities will have dire consequences.

So, what are we as Christians missing about the quarters? The revelation I received from the Lord on this subject is there are two sets of guarding angels at the four corners of the earth – one Godly the other not so much. The ones being called on the most are the ungodly ones. I believe the Godly angels set up there are for us to partner with to bring the Kingdom to earth. The vision I saw was the elemental kingdom was at one time united; and at the fall, this kingdom was split in half. This split allowed an opening for the fallen sons of God to set up outposts alongside the Godly angelic hosts who rule over these places. The occult uses the demonic angels to bring about nefarious purposes. BeliefNet, which is supposedly a Christian site, has a prayer for invoking the four archangels - Michael, Gabriel, Raphael, and Uriel. I do not recommend praying such prayers found on so-called *"Christian"* sites until you discern under what spirit the prayers were written. Uriel and Raphael are never mentioned in the Bible as being a named angel. They are, however, in the Book of Enoch.

Psalm 103:20 (AMP) refers to the mighty ones, *"Bless the Lord, you His angels, You **mighty ones** who do His commandments, Obeying the voice of His word!"* (emphasis mine). In Daniel chapter four, we read about the *"watchers"* and *"holy ones."* In verse 17, we see this statement, *"This sentence is by the decree of the angelic **watchers**, And the decision is a command of the **holy ones"*** (emphasis mine). The word for *"watcher"* in this verse is an Aramaic word and not Hebrew. It is the word *"iyr,"* which means *"angel or guardian."* This word is seen again in Jeremiah 4:16 (BRG), which states, *"Make ye mention to the nations; behold, publish against Jerusalem, that watchers come from a far country, and give out their voice against the cities of Judah"* (emphasis mine). The word for *"watchers"* here is the Hebrew word *"natsar,"* which means *"guard or watchmen."* Some translations have *"watchers"* as *"besiegers"* instead, but the original meaning is the same. This section will tie into the chapter thirteen and hopefully make more sense.

In 1 Corinthians 6:3 we read, *"Don't you know that we will judge angels? How much more the matters of this life!"* The Greek word for *"judge"* is *"krinō"* which means *"to rule, govern; to contend together, of warriors and combatants; to approve esteem, to prefer; pick out, select."* The angels are there for us to partner with.

Locking the Corners

The enemy is crafty and loves to sneak in under the Christian radar. John Ramirez writes about his time as a high-level warlock traveling to the crossroads of a neighborhood or city to "lock down the corners." This practice is performed so that the enemy has dominion over the area and possess the land. Occultists will perform blood rituals at these crossroads and make a spiritual exchange for the control of these areas. They return to these sites two times a year to reinforce the rituals.

In his book, *Unmasking the Devil*, Ramirez exposes the three reasons why the occult locks down the corners:

> *"1) if you went into a witchcraft fight with a high-ranking witch, or anyone in the witchcraft world, you already had the upper hand over the person you opposed because you already conquered that territory, so they couldn't put witchcraft on it; 2) that's how the principalities of that region, from the first and second heavens, operate – through those gateways and portals; 3) if you wanted to do witchcraft against someone, you had already locked down the person's crossroads, or his life, his community, or his travels, so you could destroy the person three ways – so if you moved to Europe, I'd still got you."*[1]

131

Scary is it not? Now, when we travel through areas where there is massive poverty surrounded by prosperity, we know how to pray. The occult chooses the crossroads as it represents all the cardinal directions – north, east, south, and west. It can also represent a person's life or the world. Witchcraft traditions believe Hecate sits at the crossroads, ready to make deals with men. She is a principality and cannot be taken head-on; however, her strongmen are greed, pride, slothfulness in business, sexual perversions. Her strongmen you can bind and remove. The blood rituals can be undone by situational repentance, and her hold will become weakened enough that she will fall.

When was the last time you went and prayed at the crossroads of your city or neighborhood? If we break the power of the enemy at the gates of our communities and towns and maintain our position of authority at those gates, we can effectively halt the advancement of the kingdom of darkness in our regions. God has empowered us to face the enemy at the gates and overcome him (Psalm 127:5, Isaiah 28:6).

Wands

Some traditions of witchcraft, such as Wicca, use wands in their practice. The purpose of a wand is to be a channeling device for power, as well as to invoke the god, goddess, or spirit of choice. It is also used in ceremonial practices in addition to blessings, charging items with energy, spell casting, and healing.

The use of wands dates back to ancient Egypt and assimilated into Wicca. A wand can be made of almost any material such as crystal, stone, wood, and metal. I have seen elaborately carved wands made from ivory. The wand can be associated to a quarter (cardinal direction) and its corresponding element. The wand's material for such alignments will depend on the elemental power being invoked. In most traditions, wands are aligned to the element of Air. Wands are predominately a male tool as it is a linear and a projective shape that is sacred to the male deity. Wands also are tied to the suit of Rod in Tarot which is linked to the element of Fire.

The wand is the ripoff of the *"mattah."* A *"mattah"* is rod or staff used in fighting, intercession, resting, and discipline. They were used to make a sound in the atmosphere. The word mattah, in the Hebrew, is masculine. There is another word for staff in Hebrew as well. It is *"mish'enah."* This word is a feminine noun that denotes the comfort aspect of a staff.

Please do not think I am telling you to go buy or make yourself a wand. This information is for you to mindful of what the enemy has stolen from us.

Tarot Cards

We have probably all seen movie or television shows of women reading the tarot cards of one of the other characters in the show. We may scoff at it and think it's all make-believe, but Tarot is a tool used by the occult for divination. There are even Tarot Card computer games and phone apps that tempt us to play so we can take a peek into our future. We may not give much credence to these things, but they are a powerful and deadly tool of the enemy.

Tarot Cards have been around for centuries and can be dated back to the 14th and 15th century Italy. The earliest known deck was crafted for the Duke of Milan around 1440. Most historical references state that Tarot Cards were an Italian storytelling game developed from an Islamic card game called *"Mamluk."* In actuality, they were developed as an evangelistic tool for spreading the religion of Mithra across Europe.

The cards underwent an evolution of sorts over the centuries. During the late 1700s and into the early 1800s a French occultist, Catholic priest, and author, Alphonse Louis Constant, under the pen name *"Magus Eliphas Levi,"* created the basis for the most popular Tarot cards still in use today. He believed in the existence of a universal *"secret doctrine of magic"* that had prevailed throughout history and was evident everywhere in the world. He also found close connections between some of the Jewish iconography and the Mithraic myths.

In 1909, A. E. White, a British member of the Hermetic Order of the Golden Dawn commissioned artist Pamela Coleman Smith to create a set of Tarot Cards that most American practitioners use today. Around the same time, known occultist Alestair Crowley developed a Tarot deck called the "Deck of Thoth" which included elements of his created religion Themla and aspects of Kabbalah. He died before the set was completed and released.

Tarot decks consist of a total of 78 cards broken into two distinct parts – the Major Arcana and the Minor Arcana. The Major Arcana, or greater secrets, supposedly tell the story of humanity's spiritual evolution into enlightenment and individuation. The cards in this group are called trump cards and consists of 22 cards without suits. This section houses the The Magician, The High Priestess, The Empress, The Emperor, The Hierophant, The Lovers, The Chariot, Strength, The Hermit, Wheel of Fortune, Justice, The Hanged Man, Death, Temperance, The Devil, The Tower, The Star, The Moon, The Sun, Judgement, The World, and The Fool. The cards from The Magician to The World are all assigned Roman numerals from I to XXI, while The Fool is the only unnumbered card. The Fool card is sometimes placed at the beginning of the deck as 0, or the end as XXII.

The Minor Arcana, or lesser secrets, represent the things that govern our day-to-day life, including practical aspects, small-scale projects, everyday relationships, etc. This grouping contains a total of 56 cards which are divided into four suits of 14 cards each. Held in the Minor Arcana are ten numbered cards and four court cards. The court cards are the King, Queen, Knight, and Page/Jack, in each of the four tarot suits. Tarot suits are swords, rods, pentacles, and cups, and each has its own meaning and supposed influence over each individual. The suits all have designated symbolisms, zodiacs, colors, elements, seasons, realms, genders, and directions.

The sword suit is symbolic of thought, challenge, and observation. This suit is aligned to Gemini, Libra, and Aquarius. The color is indigo, and the element is Air. The season of the swords suit is Winter, and the realm is the mind. The gender of this suit is male. The corresponding playing card suit is Spades. The direction is North.

The rod suit is also called the staves or wands and is symbolic of creativity, action, and passion. This suit is aligned with Aries, Leo, and Sagittarius. The color is yellow, and the element is fire. The season is Spring for the rod suit. The realm it rules is the spirit. The gender of rods is male. The corresponding playing card suit is Clubs. The direction is South.

The Pentacles suit is symbolic of health, wealth, and physical. The aligned zodiacs are Taurus, Virgo, and Capricorn. The color is green, and its element is Earth. The season is Fall. The realm is the home. The gender is female, and the corresponding playing card suit is Diamonds. The direction for this suit is East.

The suit of cups is symbolic of love, emotion, and empathy. The zodiacs for this suit are Cancer, Scorpio, and Pisces. The color for this suit is red; the element is Water, and the realm is the heart. The gender is female, and its corresponding playing card suit is Hearts. The direction is West.

Within each suit are characteristic of the strongman spirits we encounter in our daily spiritual battles. The Queen of cups card, for example, personifies the characteristics of Sofia, the Queen of the Sea, which is a manifestation of the Queen of Heaven. The nine of swords is the spirit of fear. The four of pentacles is the spirit of greed.

The occult uses these characteristics embedding in the cards to capture people under the rulership of these strongmen. Their spirits are locked into cycles of greed, depression, sexual

135

perversions, etc. based on how the tarot reader places the cards on the table in the correct combinations to create areas of bondage. It is interesting to note the layout of the Pokémon card game is the same as those of tarot cards.

I do not recommend the average Christian doing an in-depth study of the meanings behind tarot cards as it has the potential to capture the imagination. They are an effective tool of the enemy to lead many astray. Make sure you cover yourself in all research and reading on this subject matter.

If you have had a tarot reading, repent before the Lord and ask for any alignment to demonic entities to be broken off your life. Seek inner healing and deliverance to ensure no residue remains from these entrapments.

If you have practiced tarot, repent for divination and entrapping others into the demonic realms. Ask a deliverance minister for renunciations concerning divination and tarot cards.

Hexes, Curses, and Vexes

This heading may seem comical. Hollywood has done a great job of making witchcraft look either playful, sinister, or just plain dumb. When most people hear the word "hex," they either chuckle or stick their fingers out at you in a cross shape. The word *"hex"* is an American term. It is defined as *"a spell or curse, bewitching."* Sounds innocuous enough, right? The word *"hex"* dates back to the early 1800s in Pennsylvania where there were a number of German and Swiss immigrants. It came from the Pennsylvania Dutch/German word *"hexe,"* which means *"to practice sorcery or witchcraft."*

It is derived from the German word *"hexen,"* from *"Hexe"* meaning *"witch,"* from Old High German *"hagzissa;"* akin to Middle English *"hagge"* which means *"hag."*

A hex is *"the practice of casting an evil spell over something or someone."* As if there are *"good"* spells to cast on people. It can also be called a "jinx." A hex is expected to bring bad luck to the one who has been hexed. Even though a human does a hex, a demon will enact the hex. Hexes are always considered evil. Imagine that.

A *"curse"* as a noun is defined by the Merriam-Webster dictionary as *"a prayer or invocation for harm or injury to come upon one; a profane or obscene oath or word; something that is cursed or accursed; evil or misfortune that comes as if in response to imprecation or as retribution; a cause of great harm or misfortune."*

As a verb, *"curse"* means *"to use profanely insolent language against; to call upon divine or supernatural power to send injury upon; to execrate in fervent and often profane terms; to bring great evil upon."*

The first mention of the word curse occurs before the 12th century in both its noun and verb form. The word "curse" in its noun form came from the Middle English "curs," going back to Old English, meaning "a prayer that harm befalls one." The verb form goes back to the Middle English *"cursen,"* going back to Old English *"cursian"* (to swear profanely).

Witchcraft curses are usually spoken aloud, but can also be written. The Catholic church was in the habit of "cursing" people when they excommunicated them from the church. How nice of them. Christians curse each other regularly without really knowing what they are doing. Every time we speak harmful words over another person, church or ministry, leader, business, etc., we are cursing them. Ephesians 4:29 says, *"Let no harmful word come out of your mouth, but only what is beneficial for building others up according to the need so that it gives grace to those who hear it."*

We have to be mindful of our words towards others and even ourselves. We also curse ourselves when we speak negatively over our situations rather than speaking God's truth over those situations. Let the Lord reveal your misspoken words, and repent of them. Be faithful to speak blessing over others and yourself. Repent for withholding words of blessings over others and yourself.

137

Vexes are an entirely different animal. The word *"vex"* is a verb; and its meaning, according to Dictionary.com, is *"make (someone) feel annoyed, frustrated, or worried, especially with trivial matters."* So that you know, it has nothing to do with witchcraft but more to do with people poking at us. In other words, you are aggravated.

Tagging

There is a technique used in the occult that seems to confuse Christians more than anything. There are not any teaching concerning it. Even the occult does not talk about it. This technique is called *"tagging."* The occult tags people with powerful bloodlines, for retaliation, and to control. Tags are done in the spirit realm through spell casting. When a practitioner tags you in the spirit realm, it is to keep tabs on you and to have access to vex your spiritual walk. The tag will open up a channel into a person's life granting access for spells and curses to influence that individual. Some have been tagged at birth so that they would always be drawn to the occult.

Tags can also be used for spying on people. A church member or ministry partner can be walking around with a tag on them so the occult can spy on what that ministry is doing. Even a perceived wrong in the eyes of a practitioner can be grounds for them to tag a person. Perception shapes our reality. If a witch feels he or she has been wronged (even when they haven't), they can tag an individual to exact the revenge in which the witch deems appropriate.

I once knew of a witch who was a bit of a nymphomaniac. She would see someone she wanted to sleep with and tag them. She would work her spells through the tag until she was with that person. It didn't matter if it was a girl or a guy. It didn't matter if they were in a committed relationship, gay, straight, or even if they were a Christian. She would manipulate those people through the spells sent through the tag.

A tag can exist generationally as well. A witch can tag a bloodline to ensure that bloodline will live in poverty, be prosperous, enter the occult, etc. How does this happen? Someone in the bloodline comes into agreement with the tag, and it can be passed down through the generations just like a generational sin. If a tag has never been recognized in a bloodline, it will perpetuate through that bloodline. Families may think they are just jinxed not knowing they are actually tagged, allowing the enemy access to their bloodline.

Another reason the idea of tagging is so confusing for Christians is most do not believe there are any Biblical examples of this. In actuality, there is. In Romans 16:17 (KJV), we read, *"Now I beseech you, brethren, mark them which cause divisions and offenses contrary to the doctrine which ye have learned; and avoid them"* (emphasis mine). Most translations change the word *"mark"* to *"watch,"* which is only a part of the meaning of the Greek word used. The word used is *"skopeō,"* which translates as *"to look, observe; to mark; to fix one's eyes upon, to spy on; take heed."* This is, in essence, how the occult uses a tag. Now, we do not go around spying on our fellow Christians, peering through their windows and listening in on their phone conversations. We set a mark in the spirit realm on that person. That mark is intended to bring them to repentance. That is the Christian purpose of marking. Father God will remove the tag once the person comes to repentance.

Now, please hear me on this. I need to clarify what a person bringing division looks like. People who cause division are those who are spreading gossip about leaders and others in ministry, attempting to usurp a leadership position by use of slander, etc. Those who bring division to separate the goats from the sheep are **NOT** what this scripture is referring to. We are called to be discerning, but to keep that discernment in order. We discern and submit our discernment to leadership. If we perceive someone is in sin, we go to that person and speak to them (Matthew 18:15-17). We do not expose the sin or perceived sin in public or behind their backs. All correction needs to be done through love and humility (Ephesians 4:2, Galatians 6:1).

We also mark people when we bring false accusations against them. When we, say, accuse another Christian of walking in witchcraft, we are placing a label over them in the spirit realm that the enemy can see. There is now a flashing neon sign above their heads, letting the enemy know to come and annoy them. Often, those who have been accused of something will fall prey to the accusation. There are also times when the accusers will fall victim to the very sin of which they are accusing others. We only need to look at the examples of some of the major televangelists to see this modeled for us. If you have brought a false accusation against someone, you need to repent immediately. If you have any false accusations brought against you, release forgiveness towards your accusers and begin to pray blessings over those who are backstabbing you. Keep your own heart pure towards your accusers.

Scripture also says to mark those who walk uprightly. Philippians 3:17 (KJV) says, *"Brethren, be followers together of me, and mark them which walk so as ye have us for an example"* (emphasis mine). This verse uses the same Greek word for *"mark."* We are to mark those who are true examples of Christian living so we can pick up on that in the spirit and follow their example. Have you ever been strongly drawn to another believer? Maybe it is because somewhere someone marked them as a spiritual example of Christ. Could you imagine if we followed this Biblical example? If we mark those in the spirit who are Godly examples of Christ manifest on the earth, the impact of the Gospel would drastically change. I firmly believe we would see more not only coming to Christ but living as Christ's ambassadors ushering in the Kingdom on Earth. It is interesting that Philippians 3:14 uses a similar Greek word for *"mark of the high calling"* as both Romans 16:17 and Philippians 3:17. The word is *"skopos,"* which means *"an observer, a watchman; the distant mark looked at; to spy out."* The root word of *"skopeō" is "skopos."*

Tags will affect our sense of touch and at times, sight when we discern them on someone. You may hear a sound when you get close to it. Tags may have a shape to them like a dagger or a button. Make sure when you are discerning a tag on someone that you do not have any

140

preconceived notions about them.

People who have been tagged by the occult are not to be looked down on, ridiculed, or otherwise discriminated. Tagged people are no less Christian than anyone else. They need our help to be set free, and they do not require our critical judgments and gossip are. Extend to them the same grace you would want to be extended to you.

If you suspect someone has a tag, begin to intercede on their behalf. Ask the Lord to break the tag for that individual. We need to come to a place where we contend for each other's healing just as fervently as our own.

If you suspect yourself of having a tag, pray and ask the Lord. Ask someone to discern you and pray with you. It may be a situation where you need to go through inner healing to break it loose. Do not be fearful of inner healing and deliverance. There is no shame in needing and asking for help. It is a sign of maturity when you ask for help.

Practical Application 6:

With this exercise, you will be discerning a tag on each other. Take your time with this exercise as it can be difficult to discern a tag at first. Make sure you turn off all distractions before you begin. Make sure you do this with someone you trust.

➢ Begin with prayer and with worship.

➢ Have your discernment buddy sit in a chair.

➢ Ask Yeshua to allow you to feel any tags on your buddy. Take notes on how your body reacts.

➢ Ask Yeshua if He will allow you to remove the tag or if your buddy needs to seek inner healing. OBEY what He tells you. Do not try to remove a tag after He tells you not to. Removing the tag in disobedience opens you up for backlash. If you are allowed to remove the tag, do so and then ask the Father to fill the space where the tag occupied in the spirit realm with His glory.

➤ Switch places, and allow your buddy to discern you following the previous steps.

➤ **CHALLENGE:** Repeat this exercise with distractions taking notes on how it affects your discernment.

Salting

In ancient times, salt was vital. The mineral had medicinal purposes as a natural antiseptic for cleaning wounds and killing bacteria. Salt was also used to preserve food, especially in hot climates where food spoils quickly, and for flavor as it is today.

There are many superstitions surrounding salt. One of which is throwing salt over your left shoulder to prevent the devil from attacking you since he attacks from behind. This superstition is rooted in the belief that the devil detested salt due it being incorruptible and belong to God.

Some believe that spilling salt means doom or strife would befall the one who accidentally tipped over the salt container. The Koreans have a tradition of throwing salt on a person returning from a funeral in the belief that the salt would remove the dead spirits.

The Greeks would never trust anyone who did not share a bit of salt with them. Salt represented fellowship to the Greeks and was believed to be connected to the sun. Roman paid their soldiers in salt. Wars have been fought over salt.

There seems to be some significant misunderstanding concerning the use of salt being taught to the Church. Yes, the occult uses salt, but not for the purposes that some very well known speakers are teaching us. Witches use salt to cleanse, to seal, to cast circles, and for protection against evil. It is a rare case that the occult will use salt to harm someone.

Pure, non-iodized salt is used to cleanse all instruments on a witch's altar as well as to prepare the food and drink offerings made to the spirits. Practitioners believe adding iodine to salt disrupts the harmony of the salt, and therefore contaminates it. After each ritual, all instruments are scrubbed in salt and then washed.

How about taking salt baths? We soak in the tub with Epsom salt, and essential oils with candles lit around the tub. We do salt scrubs at the salon when we have our pedicures. Did you know that those are elements used in a witch's self-purification ritual? Salt has been used for centuries as a purifier by both the occult and the sons of God alike.

There are some incomplete teachings out there against the use of salt. I am not saying these teachings are necessarily wrong; they are just incomplete. And I understand their misgivings. Once we grasp the scope of how salt was used Biblically, then we will not be so quick to dismiss the use of salt.

Salt was mixed in at the creation of the incense of the Tabernacle. Exodus 30:34-35 says, *"Then Adonai said to Moses, "Take the sweet spices—stacte, onycha, and galbanum. The spices and pure frankincense are to be in equal measures. Make a fragrant mixture from them, a blend like the work of the perfumer, seasoned with salt, pure and holy."*

Salt was used as a purifier for the offerings before the Lord. Leviticus 2:13 says, *"Also you are to season with salt every sacrifice of your grain offering. You are never to allow the salt of the covenant of your God to be lacking from your grain offering. With all your sacrifices, you must offer salt."*

Salt was used for healing. 2 Kings 2:19-22 says,

"Then the men of the city said to Elisha, 'Look now, the situation of this city is pleasant, as my lord sees, but the water is bad and the land barren.' He responded, "Bring me a new jar, and put salt in it." So they brought it to him. Then he went out to the spring of water, threw salt in it and said, 'Thus says Adonai, I have healed this water. No longer will there be from there death or barrenness.' So the waters were healed to this day, according to the word that Elisha spoke."

Salt was used to create a covenant. Numbers 18:19 (AMP) says,

143

"All the offerings of the holy things, which the Israelites offer to the Lord I have given to you and to your sons and your daughters with you as a continual allotment. It is an everlasting covenant of salt [that cannot be dissolved or violated] before the Lord to you and to your descendants with you."

If you mix sulfur and salt, you get an explosive chemical reaction. This reaction is mentioned in the Bible. Deuteronomy 28:21-22 says, *"The following generation, your children who rise up after you, and the foreigner who comes from a distant land will say, when they see the plagues of that land and the sicknesses Adonai afflicted on it: 'Sulfur and salt, the whole land burnt! It cannot be planted, it cannot sprout, no grass can grow up on it—like the overthrow of Sodom and Gomorrah, Admah and Zeboiim, which Adonai overturned in His anger and in His wrath!'"* Ouch!

Let's look to the New Testament for a salt reference as well. Mark 9:49-50 says, *"For everyone will be salted with fire. Salt is good; but if the salt becomes unsalty, with what will you flavor it? Have salt in yourselves, and keep shalom with one another"* (emphasis mine).

Let me tell you this. I had a beautiful Mimosa tree in my back yard. One year, the electric company hired some people to trim (when I say trim, I actually mean butcher) the trees away from the power lines. This company tramps around my backyard and cuts my Mimosa tree down even with the ground. The stump is barely sticking up out the ground. I was not a happy camper. This company did not even ask if they could come into my back yard. The next day after my tree was gone, I went out to see the damage and lock my gate. As I stood over this blackened spot in my yard, I felt something was in my yard that was not of God. I looked up, and there was one of the work crew from this company in my yard. I glanced at the gate, and it was still locked. The worker started picking up leftover pieces of tree, and I went inside. When I looked back out my window, the guy was gone. The Lord said to take an equal measure of oil and salt, mix it, and pour it on the land where the worker had been as I prayed over my property. I didn't understand it, but I did it. I now have three beautiful Mimosa trees in my back yard all in the area where I poured the oil and salt out. It pays to be obedient.

So, do we salt or not? Listen to the leading of the Holy Spirit. If He says salt, then go ahead and salt. If He says not to, then do not salt. It is just that simple. We cannot allow misinformation to cause us to miss what the Lord has for us. Just be obedient no matter what. If you are in doubt about salt being good for the land, use Epsom salt instead. Not only is it salt, but it is also a fertilizer. It is harmless and highly beneficial to the land.

Chapter Eleven
Veils and Force Fields

The occult loves to hide things in plain sight. They get a kick out of blindsiding Christians. They will "veil" stuff so you cannot see and surround things with *"force field"* to keep you away. Why? Because they can. We will look at the purposes of both veiling and force fields in this chapter.

Veiling

"Veiling" is the act of covering with or as if with a veil. It is also known as masking. Veiling is done by the casting of spells and enchantments around their target. When occultists veil themselves, they are drawing in their aura or energy in tight into themselves. When something is veiled in the spirit realm, the item is not necessarily invisible. There has been a disconnect between what our eyes are seeing and the information being processed in our brain. The occult has figured out how to mess with our heads.

The spirits invoked or called upon to perform the veiling will vary on the caster's alignment to their deity as well as the spell used. The spell will also vary based on what is being veiled. The occult will hide places, people, and activities behind a spiritual veil that affects the natural eye. It's like the eye can see, but the brain cannot process the visual information, so, therefore, it becomes invisible. We can walk right by veiled buildings or people and never *"see"* them at all. The occult will do this so the competition can not read them. The occult will veil people, building, portals, ley lines, and ceremonial sites.

Can Christians Veil Themselves?

Yeshua did! Luke 4:29-30 says, *"Rising up, they drove Him out of the town and brought Him as far as the edge of the mountain on which their city had been built, in order to throw Him off the cliff. But passing through the middle of them, He went on His way."*

Yeshua walked right by the people, and they did not see Him at all. The Bible says we will do greater works than Jesus (John 14:12). So, it stands to reason that we too can make ourselves *"invisible"* to those around us.

How to Discern a Veil

If you suspect a place, object, person, portal or ley-line is veiled, follow these simple deductive reasoning guidelines.

- ➢ **For Locations:** Use a map. If a location is on a map, but you are unable to find it, then it is veiled. Use logic for this one.
- ➢ **For Objects:** Use your natural sense of touch.
- ➢ **For People:** Use your sense of smell. Can you smell any perfume/cologne that's not your own and no one is around you? You will have to learn how your body reacts to someone who is veiled. If you are reacting differently from an astral, then it is a good chance that the presence you feel is a veiled person.
- ➢ **For Portals, Ley-lines, Etc.:** Refer back to your journal entry as to how your body reacts to a portal and a ley-line.

Force Fields

Just like in sci-fi, a force field is a type of protective barrier around a person, place, or thing. It is generated by channeling electromagnetic energy around whatever it is they want protected. It's interesting to note that Boeing has filed for and received a patent on force field

147

technology to be used on military vehicles.

The occult practitioners will use force fields to keep trespassers out of an area or away from their person. It is done through spells and incantations. Sometimes they will put up a force field to keep something contained like demons. People, buildings, objects, vehicles and pretty much anything the occults wants to keep people away from can have a force field around it.

Some times the occult will veil Christians. Yes, the occult can veil you even if you are born again. You may not be aware that you have a force field or cage around you. The occult can manipulate the electromagnetic field around you to box you in. A force field around a person is pretty much the same thing as caging. Occultists veil or cage Christians to isolate them, to hinder the spiritual walk of Christians, to stop destiny, and to close Christians off from their gifts.

How Do You Bring a Force Field Down?

There will come a day when you will be on a prayer journey that it may be necessary to take down a force field. Be obedient to what the Lord tells you and be honest with the team leader if the Lord tells you not to touch it. Here are a few helpful strategy points to consider.

➤ First, seek the Lord to find out if it is to keep people out or something within.

➤ If it is keeping something in, ask to discern what is on the other side.

➤ Seek the Lord as to what He wants done.

➤ If the Lord says to take it down, call on the Hosts of Heaven to come and remove any entities on the other side and strip away the spells holding the field in place.

➤ If the Lord says, leave it, walk away.

How Do You Remove a Force Field from Oneself?

148

You may not be able to do this on your own. If you are uncomfortable doing this alone, seek help from a trusted deliverance minister. There is no shame in asking for help here. Look over the following strategies and take the steps necessary for your deliverance.

➤ Seek the Lord and ask if you have a field or cage around you.

➤ Fasting will help your discernment in this area significantly. Ask the Lord about a fast.

➤ If you feel that you do, ask the Lord to help you remove the field.

➤ Sometimes you may need to have another person pray with you to determine if there is a legal right for the field to be in place.

➤ Have a trusted friend discern you afterward to ensure the field is gone.

Practical Application 1:

In this exercise, you will be discerning veils. It will take some practice, so be patient with yourself. Practice does make perfect. Do this exercise as often as you like until you are fully confident in discerning a veil.

➤ Seek the Lord in prayer and lift up worship.

➤ Ask the Father to allow you to discern a veil. Take note of how your body reacts.

➤ Does it disappear after you discern it?

➤ Ask the Father if the veil needs to remain in place. If not, then ask for the Hosts of Heaven to come and rend the veil asunder and burn it in the fire of the Holy Spirit. If He says to leave it alone, then obey what He tells you.

➤ Thank Him for allowing you to discern these things.

Practical Application 2:

Your discernment of a force field will depend on how your body reacts to it. You may get all tingly the closer you get to an object or building or feel like something is pushing you in the opposite direction. The air may have a tangible feel near objects or structures. You may have the desire to leave with no real reason why. You may see them. The key is to pay attention to how you experience them. Please do this exercise with a partner and remember this is for discernment ONLY. You are not removing the force field at this time.

➤ Begin in worship and cover yourselves in prayer.

➤ Ask Yeshua to guide you in your discernment of force fields by leading you to a place with a force field around it.

➤ Take note of everything about the force field.

➤ Can you see it?

➤ Does it produce a sound?

➤ Does it push you backward or draw you forward?

➤ Ask the Father if the force field is keeping something in or something out?

➤ If it is to keep something in, ask to discern what is inside the force field.

➤ Thank Father and Yeshua for this discernment experience.

Chapter Twelve

Astrology: Stars, Planets, The Zodiac, and the Mazzaroth

In this chapter, we will discuss the elements of Astrology, which include the stars, the Zodiac, and the Mazzaroth. We may think of astrology as silly and ridiculous. We may remember reading the horoscopes at the back of magazines or in newspapers as teenagers and young adults. In our naivety, we read and believed what the horoscopes told us about our personalities. Some of what the horoscopes told us may have seemed eerily accurate. These practices have long-lasting effects which we may be unaware of. Scripture says we are destroyed from a lack of knowledge (Hosea 4:6). I hope to educate you on these practices so you can obtain deliverance and freedom.

Astronomy vs. Astrology

For as long as man has been on the Earth, we have looked up at the heavens and admired the stars. Early man traced out shapes in the night sky that resembled known animals and gave these shapes names. These shapes are called *"constellations."* Modern astronomers have recognized around 88 constellations. Most of these constellations originated with Ancient Sumerian shepherds and Mesopotamian farmers.

The constellations that are visible during Spring, Summer, Fall, and Winter are different from each other as the Earth's axis changes. There are only five constellations that are constant in the night sky all year long within the Northern Hemisphere – Ursa Major, Ursa Minor, Draco, Cepheus, and Cassiopeia. The changes in visible constellations have to do with the way the Earth is orbiting the sun during the seasons. In winter, Orion is highly visible in the Southern night sky. Scorpius is out during the day. In summer, we see the opposite; Scorpius at night and Orion are in the sky during the day. In Winter, Canis Major, Cetus Eridanus, Gemini, Orion, Perseus, and Taurus are fully visible. In the spring, the constellations of Bootes, Cancer, Crater, Hydra, Leo, and Virgo are in the night sky. In the summer, Aquila, Cygnus, Hercules, Lyra, Ophiuchus, Sagittarius and Scorpius light up the sky. In the fall, you can see Andromeda, Aquarius, Capricornus, Pegasus, and Pisces.

Jagadheep D. Pandian explains it like this in an article for The Curious Team's website "Ask an Astronomer" section:

> *"There are two major motions affecting the Earth: its rotation around its axis, and its rotation around the Sun (which we call 'revolution'). While the rotation of the Earth on its axis causes the nightly movement of the stars across the sky, the revolution is responsible for the fact that we can see different parts of the sky at different parts of the year."[1]*

Let me clarify something here. Astronomy is NOT astrology, even though the two share common roots. One is science, and the other is an occult practice. Astronomy is the study of celestial objects, space, and the physical universe as a whole. This form of science is what is referred to in the Bible as a means to tell time and seasons (Genesis 1:14-16). Astrology, on the other hand, is defined by Merriam-Webster's dictionary as *"the divination of the supposed influences of the stars and planets on human affairs and terrestrial events by their positions and aspects."*

A surprising fact is that astrology was at one time considered to be science. It is now commonly rejected as such. It is supposedly mere conjecture and speculation. We know, however, that what science cannot explain or have factual evidence on, scientists dismiss as lunacy and fantasy. They cannot account for the spirit realm at all, nor do they it have any concept of it because it does not compute with their logic. Now, I am not promoting astrology here by no means.

Berkley University writes the following on their site *"Understanding Science"* concerning astrology, *"Scientific studies involving astrology have stopped after attempting and failing to establish the validity of astrological ideas. So far, there are no documented cases of astrology contributing to a new scientific discovery."[2]*

The Bible does command us to stay way from Astrology. It is in the same category as witchcraft. Look at what Isaiah 47:13-14 says:

*"You are weary of your consultations. So many! So let the **astrologers, star-gazers, predicting by new moons**, stand up and save you from what will come upon you. Behold, they shall be as stubble. Fire will consume them. They cannot deliver themselves from the power of the flame! It is not a coal for warming by or a fire to sit before!"* (emphasis mine).

The Stars, Planets, and the Zodiac

Witchcraft practitioners view the stars as living entities in the heavens governing our lives. Their collective energies are believed to flow to the Earth and into all living things on the Earth. Rituals and festivals are all geared to follow the appearing of certain stars and constellations in the sky at certain times of the year. Specific rituals and spells require that a particular constellation is at its zenith, or highest point in the sky, for the spell to be effective. Many witchcraft traditions believe that each constellation affects a different personality trait.

The twelve Zodiac signs were birthed out of man's observation of the rotation of the sun and Earth. It was the Babylonian astrologers, and later the Greeks, initially determined zodiac signs by which constellation the sun was *"in"* on the day you were born.

Ancient astronomers noted that the majority of the stars stayed stationary with respect to each other. These stars were termed *"fixed"* stars. They observed that there were five visible stars which rotated around the Earth and confined to a narrow line. This narrow line became termed as *"the ecliptic."* This ecliptic loops around the Earth at a certain angle. Also, the Sun, the Moon, and the five visible stars all follow this same ecliptic. Astronomers divided the ecliptic into twelve sections and named them after the fixed stars.

Men observed certain events which seemed to be triggered as a planet passes through a particular section of the Zodiac. They also noted babies born under these signs displayed strikingly similar personality traits. These traits were shared by babies who were born in different years but under the same sign. Changes in these personality traits occurred when a different planet would pass through during that season as each planet rules a different domain. Based on these ancient beliefs, each planet was given its own domain that covers every aspect of human life. Each planet is said to rule the people who were born under that planet's appearing in the sky. As the planet passes through the Zodiac, they are believed to influence people in a way that would shift personalities, political powers, finances, etc.

The sun is tied to the Greek god Helios and is considered the most powerful and influential of all the ruling planets. It is believed to rule over the expression, personal power, pride and authority, leadership qualities and the principles of creativity, spontaneity, health, and vitality, the sum of which is named the life force. The sun is considered a male entity. The sun is the ruling house of Leo and is exalted in Aries.

The moon is considered the second most important of the astrological planets. It is tied to the goddess Diana. The moon is believed to rule over the unconscious habits, memories and moods, gut feelings, the urge and capacity to nurture, and the past. It is viewed as a female planet. The moon is the ruling planet of Cancer and is exalted in the zodiac sign of Taurus.

Mercury is said to rule over the mind and communication, self-transformation, and commerce. Besides watching over short-distance travel, Mercury is believed to governs all forms of communication and miscommunication. It is also considered to combine both masculine and feminine qualities. Mercury is believed to help an individual achieve reconciliation between opposing personality traits. It is believed that Mercury is the ruling planet of both Virgo and Gemini and is exalted in Virgo and Aquarius. Mercury is associated with the nervous system, the brain, the respiratory system, the thyroid, and the sense organs.

Venus is called the social planet because it is believed to rule over the principle of uniting, attraction, art & beauty, passions, and love between people. This planet is considered female and thought to rule over the female psyche. Venus is also the Roman version of the Greek goddess Aphrodite. Venus is traditionally the ruling planet of Libra and Taurus and is exalted in Pisces.

Mars is the Greek god Aries. This planet is believed to govern the outward desire, enterprise, action, self-assertiveness, anger, aggression in addition to war and implements of war and violence. People born under Mars are believed to be given to bloodlust, violence, and rage. He is called the son of Earth and is associated with unluckiness of brides. Traditionally, Mars is the ruling planet of Aries and Scorpio and is exalted in Capricorn.

Expansion, benevolence, social opportunities, exploration, widening horizons, growth, justice, wisdom, opportunity, fortune, and abundance are supposedly the domain of Jupiter. Jupiter is the Roman equivalent to the Greek god Zeus and was referred to as the *"king of the gods"* in both Greek and Roman mythology. Jupiter can also represent going to excess through over-confidence, or self-righteousness. This planet is also believed to be tied to religion, law, and philosophy. This planet is the traditional ruling planet of Sagittarius and Pisces, and it is exalted in Cancer. We know that the constellation of Cancer is directly connected to the Royal Arch Degree of Freemasonry. Jupiter is referred to as *"Guru"* or *"Brihaspati"* and is known as the *"great teacher"* in Indian astrology.

Saturn is supposedly the keeper of order and is the planet of time. Saturn is the Roman name for the Greek god Kronos. In Greek mythology, he is the son of Uranus and Gaea and one of the Titans. He lead the revolt against his father, Uranus, and became king of the gods. The planet Saturn is believed to rule over the principles of boundaries, restriction, and the giving of form. Also, the concept of reaping and sowing fall under Saturn's domain. Saturn is the traditional ruling planet of Capricorn and Aquarius and is exalted in Libra.

The planet Uranus was not discovered until 1781. Initially, Uranus was interpreted as a part of the nature of Mercury and Saturn. This planet is believed to rule over freedom, originality, sudden changes and new possibilities, the possibility of chaos, the unexpected, innovation, our desire to be unique, liberated, and radical, as well as all new technology and scientific discoveries. It is also believed that Uranus rules over societies, clubs, and any group based on humanitarian or progressive ideals. This planet rules Aquarius and is exalted in Scorpio.

In 1846, Neptune was discovered. Astrologers assigned domain of ruling over dreams and visions, self-sacrifice, charity, religion, the intangible, confusion, escapism, deception, glamour, drugs, addictions, merging or uniting, compassion, and lack of boundaries to Neptune. Both Neptune and Uranus are considered to reflect entire generations of people due to their slow movement through the ecliptic. Their effects are believed to be felt more across whole generations of society. Their impact upon individuals depends upon how strongly they feature in that individual's birth-chart. Neptune shares the rule over Pisces and its exaltation in Cancer with Jupiter.

Pluto has undergone some significant changes in the natural over the centuries. Discovered in 1930 and downgraded to a dwarf planet in 2006, Pluto is said to rule the unconscious mind, deep instincts, and the underworld. Pluto is the ruling planet of Scorpio and is exalted in Leo. Even though Pluto has been downgraded in the science community, the majority of astrologers still use Pluto as a ruling planet. Pluto is also believed to govern primary business and enormous wealth, mining, surgery and detective work, and any enterprise that involves digging under the surface to bring the truth to light. This planet is referred to as the "great renewer." It is considered to represent the part of a person that destroys to renew through bringing buried but intense needs and drives to the surface and expressing them even at the expense of the existing order.

Retrograde

Some believe that changes in the rotation of each ruling planet will affect in negative ways. The supposed change in rotation is called *"retrograde"* or *"retrograde motion."* Retrograde motion is an *"apparent"* change in the movement of the planet through the sky; however, this isn't really what is happening. A planet does not physically start moving backward in its orbit. The explanation for this apparent reversal in orbit, in our sun-central solar system, is that retrograde occurs when a faster-moving planet catches up to and passes a slower moving planet. This movement makes the usual path of a planet's east-to-west motion appear to go west-to-east. This motion can be emulated by standing side-by-side with someone you are walking with then one of you quicken your pace to pass the other. It will appear the other person is moving backward.

Astrologist will attribute everything terrible that happens with when a planet goes into retrograde. They advise people not to start anything new, to stay indoors, and to expect things to break and fall apart. There is, however, no scientific basis for these claims. Of course, we know that science cannot explain nor understand the spirit realm. There is, however, evidence of increased spiritual activity during planetary retrogrades. This occurrence is because, in the heavenly realm, gateways open as planets pass by each other, allowing entities to travel from dimension to dimension. The frequencies released by the planets, as they move, create harmonies that act as keys to open the gates. These retrograde moments would be a good time for us, as Christians, to reinforce the boundaries of our homes and territories, take spiritual inventory, and begin to eliminate anything that is displeasing to the Lord. Never dismiss an opportunity for a divine encounter with the Lord as He is revealing what is going on in the heavens.

A Second Zodiac

There is something I do need to mention here. There is another zodiac. One that most occultists will never discuss with the regular old Joe that crosses their path. Within this Zodiac reside the most evil and dark characteristics of the Zodiac and human depravity. It is called the *"Black Zodiac"* or the *"Dark Zodiac."* Just like the Western astrological Zodiac, the Black Zodiac originates from the ancient Babylonian Zodiac. This version is far more demonic than the zodiac charts we see in newspapers and magazines. The demons represented in the black Zodiac are one's inherent will and capacity to cause harm to oneself and others ultimately. Each of the twelve Black Zodiac embodies the morbid traits that are as unique as each person who is aligned with them. These demons are the foulest of the foul. Some believe these creatures are archangels who fell with Satan in his rebellion.

The Black Zodiac consists of the following:

➤ ***The Tyrant (Aries)*** – characterized by greed and an insatiable appetite; relishes in the suffering of others; sees people as tools to be used, abused, and then discarded.

➤ ***The Fallen Demon (Taurus)*** – characterized by unforgiveness and revenge; relishes in the repercussions of mistakes made.

➤ ***The Basilisk (Gemini)*** – commands fear, enjoys tormenting others, demanding respect from all; two-faced and given to gossip.

➤ ***The Serpent (Cancer)*** – characterized by wisdom mixed with deceit, cunning, cleverness, and twisting of trust to their advantage.

➤ ***The War-Maiden (Leo)*** – characterized by cruelty; appreciative of both beauty and decay; walks a thin line between evil and benign; called the evil genius of the Zodiac.

➤ ***The Maelstrom (Virgo)*** – called "the Wrath of God." This sign is characterized by violence to the one it loves most, possessiveness, a mix of jealousy and rage, and coldness.

- ➢ ***The Ravenous (Libra)*** – characterized by insanity and chaos; the loudest of the black Zodiac; sneaky and underhanded.

- ➢ ***The Poisoned Dart (Scorpio)*** – characterized by a thirst for revenge, control, and extreme patience; looks for weaknesses in others to exploit.

- ➢ ***The Tempest (Sagittarius)*** – characterized by lustful desires and impulsiveness; given to personal ambitions; seeks pleasure even at the harm of others; single focus and thinks no one else can be right.

- ➢ ***The Leviathan (Capricorn)*** – characterized by the fear of losing control; given to darkness and the sinister; desires wealth and gain at the expense of others.

- ➢ ***The Beast (Aquarius)*** – characterized by addictions to pain, fury, and despair; enjoys adding sorrows upon sorrows; loves to catch people off guard with hatred and malice.

- ➢ ***The Sword (Pisces)*** – characterized by a love to inflict hurt on others and loss of one's self in the heat of battle; a symbol of glory in battle; given to flights of fantasy.

The Mazzaroth

So, what is the Mazzaroth, and how does all of this tie in together? *"Mazzaroth"* is the Hebrew word for *"constellation"* or *"garland of stars."* We only find the word *"Mazzaroth"* mentioned twice in the Bible. But the importance of stars is very evident throughout scripture. The Mazzaroth has absolutely nothing to do with astrology or any attempt to tell our futures based on the stars.

The very first mention of the importance of stars is found in Genesis 1:14-16, which states:

> *"Then God said, 'Let lights in the expanse of the sky be for separating the day*
> *from the night. They will be for signs and for seasons and for days and years.*
> *They will be for lights in the expanse of the sky to shine upon the land.' And it*
> *happened so. Then God made the two great lights—the greater light for dominion*
> *over the day, and the lesser light as well as the stars for dominion over the night."*

The word for *"light"* is the Hebrew word *"ma'owr"* meaning *"light or luminary"* also *"candlestick."* This word can also mean *"menorah,"* and *"luminous body."* The word for "stars" is the Hebrew word *"kowkab"* which has a fascinating meaning. It means *"star – of Messiah, brothers, youth, numerous progeny, personification, God's omniscience."* It can also mean *"a prince."* Now isn't that interesting? Here is the Mazzaroth.

The Bible explains to us in Genesis 1:14 that the stars are here for signs, seasons, and for determining the days and years. In Judges 6:17, we read, *"Then he said to Him, 'If now I have found favor in Your eyes, then please, show me a sign that it is really You talking with me.'"* The word *"sign"* used in this verse is referencing the celestial bodies mentioned in Genesis 1:14. The word for *"sign"* is the Hebrew word *"owth"* and is the same word throughout the Old Testament for the word *"sign."*

I want to take a particular look at the purpose of the stars being for a sign. The constellation we know as Virgo or *"the Virgin"* is known in the Hebrew as *"Bethulah,"* also translates as *"virgin."* Bethulah is depicted with a branch in her hand. This set of stars that make up the branch are called *"Tsemech,"* which translates as *"Messiah."* This word is used in Isaiah 4:2, Jeremiah 23:5, and again in Zechariah 3:8 in reference to the coming Messiah. The Arabic names for this same constellation grouping are *"Zavijaeh"* which means *"gloriously beautiful"* and *"Al Mureddin"*, which means *"who shall have dominion."* In Chaldean, the Branch constellation is called *"Vindemiatrix"*, which translates to *"son who cometh."* The very stars themselves were a sign to point to Yeshua.

I want to go back for a moment to the stars mentioned in Genesis 1:16. Ephesians 6:12 tells us, *"For our struggle is not against flesh and blood, but against the rulers, against the powers, against the worldly forces of this darkness, and against the spiritual forces of wickedness in the **heavenly places**." (emphasis mine).*

It says *"heavenly places"* in this verse. In the Greek, *"heavenly places"* is the word *"epouranios,"* which has a variety of meanings – one of which means *"lower heavens of the stars," "celestial."*

As mentioned before, the word Mazzaroth only appears in two scriptures. The word first appears in Job 38:31-33, which states, *"Can you bind the chains of Pleiades or loosen the belt of Orion? Do you bring out the **constellations** in their season or guide the Bear with her cubs? Do you know the ordinances of the heavens? Can you set up dominion over the Earth?"* (emphasis mine).

Some translations say, *"Mazzaroth in his season"* instead of *"constellations in their season."* The Hebrew word used for *"heavens"* in this verse is *"shamayim,"* which means *"the abode of the stars"* and is called *"the expanse"* which God created in Genesis to cover the Earth (Genesis 1:8). The Hebrew word shamayim is used again in Psalm 19:2, *"The heavens declare the glory of God, and the sky shows His handiwork."* Continuing into verses three and four, David goes on to speak about how the stars and the heavens have a voice that resonates throughout the earth. The Hebrew word used for *"voice"* is *"qowl,"* which means *"sound of an instrument."* Remember NASA has recorded the sounds and songs of the planets and stars?

The second mention of the Mazzaroth appears in 2 Kings and is in a slightly different form from the first, but its meaning is the same. 2 Kings 23:4-5 (AMP) states:

> *"Then the king commanded Hilkiah the high priest and the priests of the second rank and the doorkeepers to bring out of the temple of the Lord all the articles made for Baal, for [the goddess] Asherah, and for all the **[starry] host of heaven**; and he burned them outside Jerusalem in the fields of the Kidron, and carried their ashes to Bethel [where Israel's idolatry began]. He got rid of the idolatrous priests whom the kings of Judah had ordained to burn incense [to pagan gods] in the high places in Judah's cities and all around Jerusalem—also those who burned incense to Baal, to the sun, to the moon, to the **constellations [of the Zodiac]**, and to all the **[starry] host of heaven**"* (emphasis mine).

The Hebrew word used in this scripture for *"host of heaven"* is *"tsaba,"* which means *"army, host—host of angels; of the sun, moon, and stars; those who go out to war."* This same word is echoed in Isaiah 40:26, which states, *"Lift up your eyes on high, and see! Who created these? The One who brings out their host by number, the One who calls them all by name. Because of His great strength and vast power, not one is missing."*

The word used for *"constellations"* in 2 Kings 23 is *"mazzalah,"* which is the same word as *"mazzaroth"* and translated as *"constellations - signs of the Zodiac."* From this scripture, we can deduce that there are angels, both good and evil, dwelling in the constellations. In Revelation, we are told that when Satan fell, he took a third of the stars with him (Revelation 12:4). These are the fallen Mazzaroth - the ungodly hosts.

These ungodly Mazzaroth seek to control humanity for their master, the devil. Take a look back at the Black Zodiac. When people worship the ungodly Mazzaroth, it empowers these beings and gives them the control they desire. It, in essence, traps people in time (Kronos) and space.

Look at Acts 7:41-42. It says:

> *"And they made a calf in those days, offered a sacrifice to the idol, and were rejoicing in the works of their hands. But God turned and gave them over to serve the **host of heaven**, just as it is written in the book of the Prophets: 'It was not to Me that you brought sacrifices and offerings for forty years in the wilderness, was it, O House of Israel?'" (emphasis mine).*

Did you catch that? God gave the children of Israel over to the hosts of heaven for their disobedience. The word for *"host of heaven"* is the Greek word *"stratia,"* which means *"an army, band of soldiers; troops of angels, the heavenly bodies, stars of heaven."*

We are not to be governed by the stars, but by the Spirit of God. That is why it so important for us as Christians to never look at or play with horoscopes. Our disobedience leads us into captivity. We must learn to break off the influence of the ungodly Mazzaroth that is in our generational lines.

Christian author and minister, Paul Cox, describes this principle in excellent detail in an article on his website, Aslan's Place:

> *"Picture a person connected to clock hands with the signs of the Zodiac placed in a circle like the numbers on a clock. The person rotates on the clock hands, going in circles, never getting anywhere, passed from sign to sign always the victim of the system. A victim of the mechanism which controls the hands of the zodiac clock. Wandering in the stars (Jude 13), jumping from star to star. You are not ruling and reigning. You are controlled by the mechanism, a puppet. The result of all of this is being overwhelmed, never getting anything done, always putting out fires, incompletion, repeating the same cycles, and fruitless activity. Ungodly*

seraphim seem to be in charge of this time mechanism. The worship of the stars seems to empower this system. It distorts time. This evil system says that the sons of God are not in charge of time. This seems to be their effort to change times and season. (Daniel 2:21 vs. Daniel 7:25). Instead of the godly Mazzaroth being in the times and seasons of the Lord, the Zodiac attempts to preempt God's time by having people praise (focus) on the stars (astrology) to change from God's time to the enemy's time. Therefore, there is a loss of Godly authority because you are always going in a circle."[3]

There is much misunderstanding of the stars and how we are to interact with them. God created them at the beginning (Genesis 2:1) for us. They are our weapons of spiritual warfare. Judges 5:20 says, *"From heaven, the stars fought, in their courses they fought Sisera."* Again, the word for *"stars"* is *"kowkab."* *"Courses"* is the Hebrew word *"mecillah,"* which means *"path, highway, road, or realm."* These are the righteous Mazzaroth fighting in the spirit realm against the powers behind Sisera. The Godly Mazzaroth is ours to partner within the spirit realm to do battle against the forces of darkness.

If you have ever looked at or followed horoscopes, repent immediately. Ask for others to pray for you as well to help this spirit break off you, and partner with a deliverance minister to do renunciations for disconnecting you from the stars, constellations, the Zodiac, and the ungodly Mazzaroth.

Practical Application:

Our next exercise may prove difficult at first. You will be discerning the Godly Mazzaroth. It is not an easy thing to discern the Mazzaroth as they tend to stay hidden. You will most definitely need a discernment buddy for this. You may do this from any location you feel comfortable. Again, no distractions.

➢ Enter into intimate worship with the Lord.

➤ Ask Yeshua to cover you as you worship Him.

➤ Become completely still and ask the Lord to allow you to sense the Godly Mazzaroth. Take note of how your body reacts to their presence.

➤ Ask the Lord to allow you to see the Mazzaroth.

➤ Thank Yeshua for this experience and allowing your discernment to grow.

➤ **CHALLENGE:** Repeat this exercise with distractions. Take notes on how your discernment changes when presented with distractions.

Chapter Thirteen
Pagan Holy Days

Just as we have sacred and religious holidays, the occult celebrates certain days of the year and revere them as holy. On these specific days, practitioners renew covenants and contracts, cast certain spells for the year, and honor their chosen deities. Rites performed on these days will vary with each witchcraft tradition. This chapter only covers witchcraft (Druidic, Pagan, and Wiccan) holidays, not Islamic, Catholic, or Hindu. Catholic holidays are only mentioned in the context of the *"Christianization"* of the occult holidays. I have also included prayer strategies for us to be covering ourselves with at these times.

Wheel of the Year

The observance of the seasonal cycle has been honored and observed by many cultures throughout history. Most modern witchcraft traditions follow what they call the *"Wheel of the Year."* The wheel is the annual cycle of pagan seasonal festivals or *"sabbats."* These sabbats have both Germanic and Celtic origins. Contained within the wheel are the year's two solstices and two equinoxes (solar holidays) in addition to four midpoints (Earth festivals) in between. Most pagan beliefs list the solstices as *"quarter days"* and the equinoxes as *"cross-quarter days."* Wicca tradition places more emphasis upon the cross-quarter days. The wheel consists of eight festivals broken into two groups: lesser sabbats and greater sabbats.

The lesser sabbats are Yule or Winter Solstice (December 20th through January 2nd), Ostara or Vernal Equinox (March 19th through the 22nd), Litha or Summer Solstice (June 19th through the 23rd), and Mabon or Autumnal Equinox (September 21st through the 24th). The four cross-quarter days are deeply rooted in Gaelic tradition. These festivals are Imbolc

166

(February 2nd), Beltane (May 1st), Lammas or Lughnasadh, depending on tradition (August 1st), and Samhain, pronounced sow-en, (October 31st).

As with Judaism and prophetic teachings, witchcraft believes time moves cylindrically and not linearly. The Wheel of the Year is believed to be a perpetual cycle with no beginning and no end; however, for witches, the new year begins at Samhain with other traditions believing the new year starts at Yule.

Yule

Traditionally the pagan holiday Yule is celebrated on the evening of December 20th and usually ends on January 2nd. It is also known as Yuletide and Yulefest and is celebrated as the darkness giving way to the light. Yule is also called *"Solstice Night"* as it is the longest night of the year with each day growing longer. This festival was to celebrate the rebirth of the Oak King, the Sun King, the Giver of Life. This deity is the same as the Wiccan *"Great-Horned God."* At this time of the year, Wicca believes their god (represented by the sun) is reborn of their goddess who is a representation of the Earth. Neo-pagans, Wiccans, Germanic peoples, various Northern Europeans, and LeVayan Satanists all celebrate Yule.

Some of the festivities of Yule included decorating with holly and ivy, making baskets from evergreen boughs and wheat stalks, burning of the Yule Log, going house to house giving gifts to each other, building huge bonfires, and drinking spiced cider drinks. The Yule log was usually from the Ash which represented the world tree, Yggdrasil. Revelers would also decorate with Mistletoe, which was considered to be the seeds of the divine. Druids would travel deep into the woods to harvest Mistletoe. An evergreen tree is used to symbolize immortality and the defeat of death. Many of our Christmas traditions are derived from the old Celtic and Germanic traditions.

The deities worshipped during Yule are all newborn gods, mother goddesses, sun gods, and triple goddesses. These would include Brighid, the daughter of Dagda and Dagda himself, Isis, Demeter, Gaea, Diana, The Great Mother, Apollo, Ra, Odin, Lugh, The Oak King, The Horned One, The Green Man, The Divine Child, and Mabon. This time frame would also be a rededication time for Mithra worshippers. It is also the dedication of time to Dagna.

It is noteworthy that Saturnalia takes place within the timeframe of Yule. The days of Saturnalia run from December 17th through December 23rd. This festival is also known as Kronia to the Greeks in which they honored and sacrificed to Kronos. Celebrations would include gladiator events, gift-giving, gambling, a Mardi-Gras style parade, and drunken orgies. It was also called *"The Festival of Lights."*

Yule corresponds to the Hebrew month of Tevet. This month is assigned the Hebrew letter *"ayin"* which means eye, spring/well. Chuck Pierce teaches this is the month to *"wage war against the evil eye and break the power of the evil watchers."*[1] He also suggests this is an excellent month to pray for our leaders and to fast to purify the blood so our brains and hearts can function correctly. Tevet is also the month of the tribe of Dan, and this month would be a good time to pray into our spiritual maturity and over our judgments. Tevet is also the end of Chanukah signifying there is mercy in the middle of destruction.

Prayer strategies for Yule would include renunciations for, but not limited to, Queen of Heaven, Druidisms, and Mithra. Yule is an opportune time to dedicate the time to Yeshua as the true Ruler of Time and break curses associated with generational gambling and hiding of wealth. Take the time to repent of generational anger and shame in addition to sexual sins and perversions. Ask the Father to help you refocus for this is not a time to get distracted.

Pray over your creativity and begin to ask for new flows of artistic expression in worship. Declare that the Glory of the Lord makes up your rear guard - no sneak attacks from the enemy. This month is also a time for war – a battle for the prophetic words over your life to release destiny. It is also a time to evaluate your spiritual and emotional maturity.

Imbolc

Imbolc is a Gaelic word meaning *"in the belly."* Its name comes from the time when sheep begin to give milk signifying they are pregnant. It is also called *"Brighid's day"* and the Catholic *"Saint Brigid's Day"* and *"Candlemas."* The Catholics also refer to this holiday as *"The Feast of the Purification of the Blessed Virgin Mary."* Imbolc is celebrated on February 1st beginning at sundown and runs through the entire day of February 2nd. Celebrations usually last until March 21st.

In pagan beliefs, the goddess has entered her maiden aspect, and the sun god hits puberty. According to their beliefs, this day marks the rise of Brighid's snake from the Earth to test the weather. This belief is where the modern Ground Hog day is derived. Imbolc was a day for weather divination.

This festival marks the beginning of Spring and fertility. The celebrations include honoring of maidens, the blessing of the seeds and plows, offering prayers of blessings over the livestock, the lighting of candles, maidens adorning themselves with crowns of lit candles and flowers, and cleaning out of the fireplaces and hearths. Hikes through the snow to look for signs of Spring were also incorporated in the festivities.

This festival falls within the month of Shevat. The Hebrew letter assigned to this month is *"tzadik"* which is symbolic of the *"righteous one"*[1] and is the month of Asher. Asher means *"happy, blessed."*

Prayer strategies would include praying for righteousness to be your foundation and declare blessings are on the way. Declare God's provision over every aspect of your life. Put your focus squarely on God during this time. Taste and see that He is good. Be mindful of who you are allowing to speak into your life during this time as well. Take the time during this month to plan and strategize with the Lord about your future generations. Consider a Daniel fast during this time.

Renunciations would include, but not limited to, Queen of Heaven, Druidism, and Roman-Catholic. Repentance for generational weather divination and misandry (the hatred of men and boys) would also be a good idea.

Ostara

Ostara is all about fertility. This quarter-day is also known as *"Lady Day"* or in Druidic traditions as *"Alban Eiler."* The time frame for this festival falls between March 21st and March 22nd. This festival is all about fertility, new birth, and female power. This festival is linked to Aphrodite, Ishtar, and is tied to the deity *"Eostra."* Her name is where we derive the word *"estrogen."*

Symbols used during this month are the hare (which is associated with fertility and madness), eggs, daffodils, and snakes. This time is revered as the divine marriage of the goddess and the god in paganism. Ostara is celebrated with planting seeds, feasting, and *"fun."* Elements of Ishtar worship have mingled into Ostara such as the hot cross buns. Any of this sound similar to a certain Christian holiday?

This festival falls within the Hebrew months of Adar and Nissan depending on where the new moon falls. Adar is given the Hebrew letter *"kuf,"* which represents the removal of the masquerade mask and entering into joy. Adar is associated with the tribe of Naphtali, whose name means *"my struggle, my strife."* Nissan's letter is *"hei,"* which depicts fresh wind, breath, and praise. Nissan is associated with the tribe of Judah, which means *"praise."* Adar is the time for the Feast of Purim and the Esther fast. Nissan is Passover month.

Good prayer strategies for us would be to pray against mental anguish and turmoil, ask the Father to preserve your seed (both financial and generational, aka children), and be praying that the mask of deception to be removed. This time would also be an excellent opportunity to have an inner healing session.

Renunciations may include, but not limited to, Roman Catholicism, Queen of Heaven, Kundalini, Druidism, Mithra, and Freemasonry. Ask for a renewal of your praise to our Heavenly Father. The transition period between these two months would be a great time to seek the Lord for a fresh revelation of your spiritual identity. Take some spiritual inventory and remove what is displeasing to the Lord so that renewal can come.

Beltane

Beltane runs from sundown on April 30th and goes through sunset of May 1st. It is a day the occult celebrates life and sex. It is also called the "Fire Festival" after the Celtic deity Bel whose name means *"bright one"* and *"goodly fire."* This is considered the first of the two-spirit nights; the second is during Samhain. Pagans believe that the veil between the spirit realm and the natural world is at the thinnest point and time and space laws are no longer in effect.

Maypoles crafted from Birch trees were erected to represent the male deity. A large ring of greenery and flowers were slipped over the top of the pole as the symbol of the female deity's fertility. A variety of colored ribbons were draped downward from the ring. The ensuing weaving dance symbolizes the spiral of Life and the union of the Goddess and God, the union between Earth and Sky. Human sacrifices were also made during Beltane.

All hearth fires were doused before a huge bonfire was lit for all to come to and dance. Torches were lit from the bonfire and carried home to relight the home fires. Celebrations would include jumping over a fire as a means of purification. Couples would jump together as a means to renew their commitment to each other. Cattle may be run through the smoke as a means of warding off disease and increasing their fertility. This festival was also considered an excellent time to get married. Sexual activities were always incorporated in the celebrations of Beltane. Married and single people alike were encouraged to enact the union of the god and goddess.

This festival falls in the Hebrew month of Iyar, the month of Issachar. Issachar means *"his reward will come."* The Hebrew letter for this month is *"vav,"* which symbolizes connections and linking. This will be a time to receive and understand Divine spiritual secrets. The month of Iyar is also called *"Ziv,"* which means *"radiance."* This month is associated with healing and transition. The tribe of Issachar was those with the ability to discern the times and seasons of the Lord.

Prayer strategies would include praying for your marriage and rededicating it to the Lord, praying over your mind, asking for increased discernment, and asking for God to reveal His secrets to you. Pray over your dream life as well. Ask for God's holy fire to burn anew in you. Renunciations would include, but not limited to, Druidism, Baal worship, and Necromancy. Repent for generational and personal sexual sins and sexual idolatry. This month would also be a prime time to seek inner healing. Begin to declare that the Lord is your reward.

Litha

This festival is celebrated on the longest day of the year (June 20th) and the shortest night. Pagans believe that the god is in his full power during this time, and the goddess is bringing forth the harvests. There is a focus on the element of fire in honor of the sun deity and to Pan. Any deities of the sun, harvest, animals, fertility, and the earth are worshiped at this time. This sabbat is a time for gathering herbs for medicine, magic and harnessing male energies. It is also a time when practitioners would rededicate themselves to the *"Lord and Lady"* and their particular traditions. Litha is also a time in which the pagans believe fairies come out to frolic with humankind.

All celebrations for this sabbat are done at noon when the sun is at its highest point. Festivities include community picnics consisting of fresh fruits and vegetables, nature walks,

172

making decorations from oak leaves and branches, crafting spicy incense, drinking of mead, and bonfires by night set upon high hills.

Depending on the new moon, Litha can fall within the Hebrew months of either Sivan or Tammuz. The month of Sivan is the month of Zebulun with the letter *"zayin,"* which is representative of receiving mercy for completion. Zebulun means *"to dwell,"* and this month is the time of Pentecost. Tammuz is the month of the tribe of Simeon with the letter *"chet."* Chet means *"light radiating from the eyes."* Reuben means *"behold, a son."*

Prayer strategies for this time would include asking God's protection over giving and businesses. Reset the boundaries of your home and property during this time. Take the opportunity to do a check-up on your talk vs. walk. Also, be mindful of what you are looking at and ask the Father to cleanse your eye gates. Make assessments of your spiritual progress and renew your covenant with the Lord.

Renunciations would include, but not limited to, Wicca, Druidism, Royal Arch Degree of Freemasonry, and any generational sun worship (includes First Nations). Break covenants made to the false deities of Wicca and Paganism. Renounce all witchcraft practices. Break off the shell of hardness from off your heart. Retune your worship.

Lammas / Lughnasadh

The name Lammas means *"loaf mass."* This holiday is also called Lughnasadh. It translates into the funeral games of Lugh. These games were to honor Lugh's mother. Lugh was the Celtic deity of craftsmen. Traditionally, this holiday is celebrated on August 1st.

This pagan sabbat celebrates the first grain harvest. The worship of the goddess in her mother state is the primary focus for Wicca and Neo-pagans. Worship rites will follow those for Demeter and Ceres. Produce, and grain offerings would be placed on altars for the spirits.

This festival includes harvesting, circle dancing that mirrors solar rotation, bread making, and crafting decorations for the home. Marriage was encouraged during Lammas celebrations as well. The first sheaf of wheat, barley, or oats collected would be ground into flour and made into bread for the whole community to share. A community potluck would be held during this time to share in the bounty of the fields and gardens. Corn dolls would be fashioned from the last sheaf of wheat harvested and carried throughout the villages. If it had been a great harvest, the dolls were fashioned to appear as maidens. If a bad harvest occurred, the dolls were made to look like hags. These dolls would *"live"* in homes above the fireplace until the next harvest.

Magic would be on the increase during this sabbat. The very first loaves of bread baked were blessed and distributed for people to take and break into four equal parts that would be placed in the four corners of their barns as a means of protection. Protection spells would be cast over homes as well. It is a time when the Wiccans will perfect their nature magic.

This festival falls in the month of Av. Av is for the tribe of Simeon. Simeon means *"to hear; be concerned."* The letter for this month is *"tet"* which resembles the womb. Av is a time when *"the secret of pregnancy is made manifest in the earth realm."*[1] This will be a time when the divine will of the Father is carried out. This month is the timeframe to stand your ground with the enemy and mix faith with the promises of God for your life. Take time to celebrate the goodness of the Lord.

Good prayer strategies for us would be to proclaim God's promises over our lives, ask for a cleansing of our discernment and realign how we hear, and break off discouragement, depression, and unbelief. Take the opportunity to sow a Firstfruit offering. Be listening for the roar of the Lion of Judah that will give you a breakthrough for the coming month. Pray over your choices so that you will choose God over situations that present themselves and the judgments of man. Cover your sound in prayer. Ask for help resetting your sound. Also, study over Psalms 32.

Renunciations would include, but not limited to, Druidism, Wicca, Queen of Heaven and generational pride. Offer repentance for generational squandering of financial harvests and theft of Firstfruits, in addition to corruption of your sound.

Mabon

Mabon is the celebration of the son of the goddess. He is called *"the child of light."* This sabbat is the time of the second harvest. The Autumn Equinox (September 21st through September 24th depending upon tradition) is when both the night and the day are the same length. It is believed to be the perfect balance of male and female energies. This festival is a time of rest after the labor of the harvest.

The Druids called this day *"Mea'n Fo' mhair"* and honored the god of the forest called *"the Green Man."* Wiccans honor the goddess as she passes into the crone stage. Mabon has also been called *"The Feast of Avalon."* Deities honored during Mabon are the goddesses Modron, Morgan, Epona, Persephone, Pamona and the Muses, and the gods Mabon, Thoth, Thor, Hermes, and The Green Man.

Celebratory activities include making wine, gathering dried herbs, plants, seeds, and seed pods, walking in the woods, scattering offerings in harvested fields, giving drink offerings to trees, adorning burial sites with leaves, acorns, and pine cones to honor those who have passed

175

over. Spells for protection, prosperity, security, self-confidence, and for harmony and balance are cast during Mabon. Planting of bulbs that bloom in early spring are part of the Mabon traditions as well as taking walks in nature, and cleaning out.

Mabon falls within the month of Tishri. The tribe of Ephraim is assigned to Tishri. Tishri is the time of the Feast of Trumpets, Atonement, and Tabernacles. Ephraim means *"be fruitful and multiply."* The Hebrew letter for Tishri is *"lamed"* which *"signifies the aspiration to return to your Absolute Source."*[1] Tishri is the head of the year according to the Jewish calendar.

Some prayer strategies to consider would be to make the declaration of God as your source. Begin to declare that you are entering into Kairos time and stepping out of Kronos. Pray for spiritual awakening and increase. This season would be an excellent time to ask the Lord to do some spiritual pruning by asking Yeshua to remove anything that would hinder your intimacy with Him. Ask for an increase of revelatory knowledge. Dedicate the coming year to the Lord. Renunciations for this time would include, but not limited to, Druidism, Wicca, Leviathan, Freemasonry, Germanic Heathenry (Viking), and Queen of Heaven. Pray to have all of your scattered pieces returned, cleansed in the blood of Yeshua. Repent of any personal and generational bitterness.

Samhain

Samhain is the darkest of the occult holidays. It is the satanic high holy day of the year. This sabbat runs from sundown on October 31st and ends at sunset on November 1st. This festival is also known as *"All Souls Night," "Feast of the Dead," "Festival of Remembrance," "Feast of Apples,"* and *"New Year."*

The name Samhain means *"end of summer"* and is marked by the last harvest of the year. Pagans believe, at this sabbat, a temporal hiccup happens causing the laws of time and space to be suspended, and the veil between the worlds is at its thinnest. Samhain is a time of

Necromancy. On Samhain, pagans believe the spirits of the dead roam the earth freely tormenting or communing with whom they please. Food and drink offerings to the spirits of the dead are placed on altars surrounded by lit candles. Cattle were traditionally slaughtered on Samhain for food during the coming winter months.

Celebrations of Samhain include cemetery visits, taking midnight strolls with spirits, Necromancy, sexual perversions, feasting, divination, spell casting, and sacrifices. Human, animal, and crop sacrifices are also done on this day. Sexual acts of indecent nature are performed on this night. During this time, demonic activities are at their height, and it is said that spells are at their most potent. Prayers will be offered to the dark god and goddess.

Samhain falls in the Hebrew month of Cheshvan which is associated with the Hebrew letter *"nun"* and the tribe of Manasseh. *"Nun"* symbolizes the Messiah. Manasseh means *"to forget, to leap, up and away."* Take this time to analyze what we have heard. It is also a time to watch our words and to stand in our authority. It was during the month of Cheshvan that the flood began and also ended the following year.

Strategies are to pray into a fresh revelation of your authority, set a watch over your mouth so you will not sin against God, ask for a fresh outpouring of the Holy Spirit in your life, proclaim you are leaping up in the things of God, pray for deep revelation of the Word and teaching you have heard. Pay close attention to whose image you are presenting to others – yours or Christ's.

Release prayers of protection over your home, family, finances, health, and ministry as these are areas the occult will be going after during Samhain. Renunciations to revisit would include, but not limited to, Druidism, Satanism, Wicca, Necromancy, divination, generational sexual sins and perversions, voodoo, Santeria, shame and abandonment, and Freemasonry sexual abuse.

Chapter Fourteen
Walking in the Light

For years I lived in shame. Shame of the few years I spent slithering around in the darkness. Even though Yeshua set me free from that life, there was still a burden to carry of how others viewed me. I was caught in the trap of the fear of man. I was terrified of people finding out about me being involved in witchcraft, especially those of the household of faith. I knew how judgmental church folks could be. All of that religious dogma would flat out reject everything I have to offer based solely on their perception of me. Churchy people tend to throw the baby out with the bathwater when it comes to those who have a dark past. It seems that a murderer would have a better chance of being accepted than those of us who God liberated from Hell's grip. I tried to overcome it, sought inner healing for it. I did the renunciations for shame and rejection. I did the renunciations for fear. I have spent hours upon hours in inner healing sessions that were rather uncomfortable and painful. I still was stuck wondering what people thought about my past.

When I was asked to write this book, I did not want to. I did not want to look back at what God had delivered me from. I felt I would be looking full-face into the evil God had so graciously delivered me from. I struggled with it. Even though I had only served the darkness for a short time, it was still a very shameful experience for me. I know some have a more shameful past than turning to the occult. Even though I had undergone multiple inner healing sessions concerning my past and my bloodline being drawn to the occult, I still carried shame over my past.

Then it hit me. One Wednesday night at church, the worship team was singing *"Glorious Day"* by Kristian Stanfill. The Lord told me I was looking at this book all wrong. These lyrics of this song rang out and resonated in my very soul - *"You called my name; Then I ran out of that grave; Out of the darkness; Into Your glorious day."*[1] Lightbulb moment! He called me out of that darkness by name, and I am now standing in His light. I can look back at that part of my life with Yeshua standing by my side, showing me how He had me the entire time. He knew all about my dark years, saw everything I did, and still chose me. The shame broke and ran for cover!

I am seated with Yeshua in heavenly places (Ephesians 2:6). That truth took a bit of time to sink in. There are days I still struggle with that truth, but I am coming into my authority. I can hold my head high, stand tall, and proclaim that I was a witch that God redeemed by His Son, Yeshua. I am unashamed of my past. *I AM MORE THAN MY PAST!* What I experienced, God is changing into weapons of war to storm the gates of Hell and liberate the captives! I am a warrior. I am a daughter of the Most High God, a daughter of the King! I am more than an overcomer and am more than a conqueror through Christ!

I have been accused of still carrying witchcraft and operating therein. I have been accused of being tagged by the occult and having witches watch and manipulate everything I say and do. You know what, let them talk and accuse. I know who I am and whose I am. Yeshua stands as my advocate and my kinsman-redeemer. I know what He redeemed me from, and NO ONE can take that from me! So, I let people talk and whisper because that is what people do. I do not hold anything against any of them. My identity is not found in the minds, mouths, and hearts of others; it comes directly from my Heavenly Father.

I know I may not be perfectly polished, but I am pressing on toward the goal for the reward of the upward calling of God in Messiah Yeshua (Philippians 3:14). I am still growing and developing into who He has called me to be. I am still going through deliverance and inner healing so I can be the best version of myself that I can be. I am walking in His light now, and I intend on staying there.

I can say this for sure, since writing this book, I have fallen more in love with my Savior now than ever before. I have a new appreciation for what He has done for me, through me, and in me. The joy of my salvation is ever-present. I have hope for the future and excitement. I cannot wait for the next part of this journey.

References:

Unless otherwise noted, scripture references are from the Tree of Life Version of the Bible.

Introduction:
1 Pierce, Chuck. 28 June 2018. *"The Sense of Hearing: Four Dimensions of Hearing God"* [Video]. *https://youtu.be/qp-cqjqf8MI* (Retrieved May 4, 2019).

Chapter One:
1 Liardon, Roberts. (1997) *Sharpen Your Discernment: Because When Life Looks Grey, It's Really Black and White.* Tulsa, Oklahoma: Albury Publishing. (pp. 38)

2 Stevens, Kevin. *"I AM Activating Spiritual Senses."* His Kingdom Prophecy. 15 August 2016. *https://www.hiskingdomprophecy.com/i-am-activating-spiritual-senses/* (Retrieved May 9, 2019)

Chapter Two:
1 Wagner, C. Peter. (2012) *Discover Your Spiritual Gifts.* Bloomington, MN: Chosen Books. (p. 63)

2 Anosike, Pedro. *"Discernment and Gift of Discernment of Spirits."* 3 June 2012. © 2012 Pedro Anosike. *http://www.pedroanosike.com/discernment-and-gift-of-discernment-of-spirits/* (Retrieved May 4, 2019)

3 Cox, Paul. *"Training Your Senses: The Gift of Discernment."* 26 June 2013. *http://aslansplace.com/language/en/training-your-senses-the-gift-of-discernment/* (Retrieved May 2, 2019)

Chapter Three:
1 Pierce, Chuck. 28 June 2018. *"The Sense of Hearing: Four Dimensions of Hearing God"* [Video]. *https://youtu.be/qp-cqjqf8MI* (Retrieved May 4, 2019).

2 Ramirez, John. (2017) *Armed and Dangerous.* Bloomington, MN: Chosen Books. (p. 115).

3 Backus, David. *"The Thing With Discerners"* 11 November 2011. © 2019 The Free Believers Network, *http://freebelievers.com/fbnblog-entry/the-thing-with-discerners* (Retrieved June 6, 2019).

Chapter Three (cont'd):

4 Calder, Helen. *"Seer or Discerner: What is the Difference?"* 19 July 2017. © Helen Calder, Enliven Blog – Prophetic Teaching, h*ttps://www.enlivenpublishing.com/blog/2017/07/19/seer-or-discerner-what-is-the-difference/* (Retrieved June 4, 2019)

Chapter Four:

1 Smart Vision Labs, *"Why Vision Is the Most Important Sense Organ."* 30 June 2017. © Smart Vision Labs. *https://medium.com/@SmartVisionLabs/why-vision-is-the-most-important-sense-organ-60a2cec1c164* (Retrieved June 11, 2019).

Chapter Six:

1 Fazekas, Thomas. *"Why Your Self-Identity Is Important."* © 2018 Freedom From Limiting Beliefs. *http://www.freedomfromlimitingbeliefs.com/self-identity-is-important/* (Retrieved July 3, 2019).

2 Hyatt, Eddie. *"What You Need to Know About the Powerful Women Who Helped Ignite the Azusa Street Revival."* 12 April 2018. © 2019 Charisma Media. *https://www.charismanews.com/us/70530-what-you-need-to-know-about-the-powerful-women-who-helped-ignite-the-azusa-street-revival* (Retrieved August 2, 2019).

3 Nicloy, Major Scott. *"Spiritual Abuse."* February 2006. ©2006 The Salvation Army. *http://www.micsem.org/pubs/counselor/frames/spiritabuse.htm* (Retrieved July 19, 2019).

4 Heitzig, Skip. *"The Harmony of Submission."* 28 May 2015. ©2015 Skip Heitzig. *https://billygraham.org/decision-magazine/june-2015/the-harmony-of-submission/* (Retrieved June 17, 2019).

5 Merritt, William. *"Generational Iniquity."* 25 March 2015. © Bloom Built. *https://dayone.me/1y3Xzqi* (Retrieved July 19, 2019).

Chapter Seven:

1 Smith, Paul H., *"What is Remote Viewing?"* © 2019 IRVA. *https://www.irva.org/remote-viewing/definition.html* (Retrieved June 6, 2019).

Chapter Eight:

1 Blavatski, Helena, *"Hierachies"* as published in *Collected Writings Volume 12, Instructions II.* Publication date and publisher unknown. (p.526).

2 Sadeghi, Habib, Dr. and Sami, Sherry, *"Dr. Forgotten Genius: Royal Raymond Rife."* 28 August 2017. © Be Hive of Healing Medical Corp. *https://behiveofhealing.com/forgotten-genius-royal-raymond-rife/* (Retrieved August 8, 2019).

3 Thomson, Bill. *"Cancer & Sound."* ©2019 Delamora Transformational Experiences. *https://www.delamora.life/sound-therapy/cancer-sound-healing* (Retrieved August 8, 2019).

4 Horowitz, Leonard, Dr. *"Musical Cult Control."* 7 May 2015. © 2015, Medicalveritas.com. *https://medicalveritas.org/musical-cult-control/* (Retrieved August 8, 2019).

5 Pigeon, Ir. Stephanie, Dr. *"Ut, Re, Mi, Fa, Sol, La, Si..."* © 2013-2019 Dr. Ir. S. Pigeon • myNoise bvba. *https://mynoise.net/NoiseMachines/solfeggioTonesGenerator.php* (Retrieved August 8, 2019).

6 Lehar, Steven. *"Harmonic Resonance In The Brain: Spatial Patterns in Perception and Behavior Mediated by Spatial Standing Waves in Neural Tissue."* © 2019 Steven Lehar. *http://cns-alumni.bu.edu/~slehar/HRezBook/HRezBook.html* (Retrieved August 8, 2019).

7 Switchfoot. Lyrics to "Native Tongue." *Native Tongue,* 2018, https://genius.com/Switchfoot-native-tongue-lyrics © Highest Music.

Chapter Nine:

1 Amsden, Dr. Patti. (2007). *Portals: Releasing the Power and Presence of God into the Earth.* Collinsville, Illinois. Patti Amsden Ministries. (p. 8).

2 Cox, Paul & Parker, Barbara Kain. (2015). *Exploring Heavenly Places, Volume 3: Gates, Doors, and the Grid.* Apple Valley, CA. Aslan's Place Publications, (p. 63).

3 Amsden, Dr. Patti. (2007). *Portals: Releasing the Power and Presence of God into the Earth.* Collinsville, Illinois. Patti Amsden Ministries. (pp.112).

4 Wikipedia. *"Well Poisoning."* 9 February 2019. *https://en.wikipedia.org/wiki/Well_poisoning* (Retrieved March 20, 2019)

Chapter Nine (cont'd):

5 Wikipedia. *"Poisoning the Well."* 23 June 2019.
https://en.wikipedia.org/wiki/Poisoning_the_well (Retrieved July 8, 2019).

6 Amsden, Dr. Patti. (2007). <u>*Portals: Releasing the Power and Presence of God into the Earth.*</u>
Collinsville, Illinois. Patti Amsden Ministries. (p. 114).

Chapter Ten:

1 Ramirez, John. (2015). "<u>Unmasking the Devil</u>." Shippensburg, PA. Destiny Image
Publishing, (pp. 112-113, 115),

Chapter Twelve:

1 Pandian, Jagadheep D. *"Why Do Different Stars Appear with Seasons?"* 28 June 2015. ©
1997 - 2019 The Curious Team. https://bit.ly/2FvF94P (Retrieved July 24, 2019).

2 The University of California Museum of Paleontology, Berkley. *"Astrology: Is it scientific?"*
Understanding Science © 2019 by The University of California Museum of Paleontology,
Berkeley, and the Regents of the University of California.
https://undsci.berkeley.edu/article/astrology_checklist# (Retrieved July 24, 2019).

3 Cox, Paul. *"Zodiac and Time."* 18 May, 2019. © 2019 Aslan's Place.
https://aslansplace.com/language/en/zodiac-and-time/ (Retrieved July 25, 2019)

Chapter Thirteen:

1 Pierce, Chuck. (2011). "<u>A Time to Advance</u>." Denton, TX. Glory of Zion International, Inc.,
(pp. 312, 317, 281, 298).

Made in the USA
Columbia, SC
28 February 2020